Guilty
America's Conquest

by

Norman Garrett

DORRANCE PUBLISHING CO., INC.
PITTSBURGH, PENNSYLVANIA 15222

Dorrance Publishing Co., Inc.
701 Smithfield Street
Pittsburgh, PA 15222
Visit our website at *www.dorrancebookstore.com*

ISBN: 978-1-4349-1661-7
eISBN: 978-1-4349-1674-7

Guilty
America's Conquest

by

Norman Garrett

Contents

Foreword

At the beginning of this unfortunate episode, I discussed the impact of Ronald Saginaw's remarks about the physical reality that everybody in prison was guilty, but I knew I was not. Although my appeal was denied, I was yet to prove that not only Ronnie was wrong about all of us, the inhabitants, but I would also prove my appeal decision was also very wrong and that the federal judge who presided over the appeal would vacate the same conviction the judge had upheld six weeks earlier, and I would leave Ronnie, Al, Pete, and Reggie, and all the others behind in Kentucky within five months since I first arrived. But I took with me the thoughts and memories of them and I promised that I would help them in any way I could, if not soon but in the future.

This story is dedicated to my constant perseverance to survive in an unjust and different world and to prove how the government conspires and frames its citizens, and to expose the *sua sponte*, sinister, and manipulative measures they would undertake to prove they are always right and that they must be the victor at all and at any cost even if it means the loss of life of the accused.

This story is also dedicated to the people who inspired and supported me in my successful quest to reveal the truth about the evil empire of the law enforcement branch of the federal government.

It is also dedicated to my family who supported me in the best way they could, and to my wife Arlene who suffered through it all. It was a quest but at a high price. I lost my marriage, my career, and almost became homeless and penniless, but I survived through the mercies of God.

It is also dedicated to Patricia to whom I never had the chance to say thank you for her support because, although she knew I was coming home, she died the day before my return, which was intentionally delayed by the government.

Finally, it is dedicated to the people in prisons in all the Americas, North and South, and all over the world due to the oppression by the enforcers in their evil empires.

Never would I have thought that I would share in my area of confinement members of the underworld, specifically an octogenarian, one of the Chicago mob bosses who infiltrated the Las Vegas gambling industry in the past decades, and who knew Al Capone according to information by F.B.I. sources. I even shared the company of an inmate that came in two months before I left. This guy flew home every Friday to Alabama from his Wall Street job. He was convicted in the junk bonds scandal of the 1980s. He had a colonoscopy problem. Names of characters have been altered to protect their identities. Names of actual characters are well documented in the annals of the American criminal justice systems.

Guilt and Innocence

I was lying on my bed reading and researching. I was searching for any reason I could find concerning our so-called criminal justice system, when Ronnie said out loud, "Everybody in here is guilty." Guys jumped to their feet. Other inmate visitors from other sections of the unit screamed at such an outlandish remark by another inmate. My bed was directly across from Ronnie and between the ten-foot walkway that separates the bunks on both sides of the walkway. I was in a hospital position on my bed with the head section raised, and I turned left and glanced at Ronnie who had his eyes in a magazine when he made that remark. Ronnie had been in the system three years full time with twelve to go, except for Antonio of mob affiliations who had more years to go. No one dared challenge Ronnie on such a blatant remark. Someone told me that if this was a "real prison" instead of a prison hospital, such a remark could result into a full blown argument, a fight, or even death. The remark in itself reflects on the true existence of the facility and the reason for its occupants, the prisoners. That's why they are there. They are a bunch of fucking criminals.

For a moment there my brain went through an instant scan to find a clear logic behind Ronnie's remark. Then I knew the answer.

Ronald Saginaw is the type of guy who made jokes and spoke about prisons especially to newcomers and those with little tenure in the prison system.

He would speak about actions and reactions by different prisoners of different facilities. He spoke about recourses and reprisals. Ronnie only spoke to people he appreciated and they were very few. Most of the time he did not speak, but we spoke a lot together. At times he would continue to say to me, "You don't belong here."

The inmates started to argue between themselves and began to present their opinions on such a remark, but made no confrontations with Ronnie. I smiled and looked up at Ronnie who raised his head slowly and looked up just enough for me to see his nose above the top of the book that he was reading. He put the book down when he realized that he was being observed because everyone was still in shock. Smilingly, he calmly said out loud the logic behind the remark, the very logic my scanned brain had produced, "You either plead guilty or found guilty," and he said it loud with that southern accent. Ronnie had a stroke in a Springfield Missouri prison about two years ago prior to being here in Kentucky. His tongue sometimes comes out of his mouth while forming the words. Now through his protruding eyeglasses and also with now a more stern and serious look from that wry smile, he remarked, "There is no one in here that is not guilty."

Now I started to laugh. He continued, with widening eyes and as serious as he could, "Some of you all may feel you are not guilty, like you were framed, or lack of evidence, the judge did not instruct the jury properly, your lawyer did not dwell on all the facts, ineffective counsel or whatever the reason." He paused, and now he is going all the way, "The bottom line is, you are here, and I have never heard of anyone who was not guilty that was in jail. So there is no reason to moan and groan. All of us is guilty." Then he smiled when he said looking straight at me, "I don't know about misdemeanors, but you all did something or somebody said you did something, that is why you were fucking put here." Everybody got quiet and I kept laughing. Soon the visitors and the other inmates in the dormitory decided that not only laughing was the best way to deal with Ronnie's remarks, but the laugh had the irony behind it and that the remark was a hundred percent true, and that they were facing the real truth of their present existence. But, is everybody guilty as Ronnie said?

They may be guilty as far as being in a federal prison in Lexington Kentucky. But are they guilty as charged?

This is a true story of a man not only imprisoned unjustly, but was abused by the criminal justice system and the plaintiff, the federal government who was also his employer.

In this particular case, the employer, the plaintiff, and the criminal justice officials are all one and also are agents of federal government.

The defendant's attorney was a federal public defender, who is another officer for the federal government. I guess you are beginning to smell something. That's right, "conspiracy," and a definitive dead end for me, the defendant.

In part, Ronnie was right about the reality of the present physical circumstances. I was yet to prove to him about idealism, reality of a different kind, truth, and most of all, challenge, that changed my physical circumstance at Lexington, but at a terrible price.

I was about to put the criminal justice system to a test, and by their own guidelines. In other words, the criminal justice system was put on trial by a misdemeanor.

The Visit

The past thirty years since I had become an adult, the word "visit" meant going to the capital, another village, town or another countryside of the tropical country of my birth, which I visited this past few years conveniently because I could not work as I did before. I was injured working for whom? Well, you guess it again—Uncle Sam. People travel from all over the country to other parts of the country and all over the world visiting, and there are people who receive visits at the prisons.

My first visit to a prison was when I became a prisoner and my first involuntary plane trip was when I was taken to Lexington Kentucky on February 13, 1996. This trip was not for me to see the derby preparation, but to spend a year at a prison on a concocted, planned, conspired twelve-month prison sentence. I was no ordinary prisoner, but in reality I was one. I arrived at Bluegrass Airport on an eight-seater prop plane. I was never in such a small plane and was very scared during the flight when the plane kept rising and dropping through the clouds like a bird. I thought it was the end of me. My legs were never shackled due to my inability to walk. The airplane marshal had started to get a bit worried because I used the bathroom three times. He did not know I had a urinary problem. With one hand free to hold my cane and the left hand cuffed to the chain around my waist, he put a second cuff to limit any left hand movement. Maybe he thought I might try something like freeing one of the three other prisoners and my right hand would be inadequate to do so. I was the only visitor for Kentucky; the others went to Rochester, Minnesota and Springfield, Missouri. They were two males, one white and one Asian female, all bound hand and feet. I was helped off the plane at eleven in the morning during arrival. Two Kentucky marshals, one female, were there to pick me up. I sat with the female in the car for about ten minutes, while the other marshal went on board and chatted with the marshals, including two male pilots and one female.

On the plane, I asked her what the prison was like. Her only reply was that I would be assigned a bed in the hospital. Later I would find out this was no hospital, but a third-rate medical facility as it is called. It is a medical facility with a humongous industrial complex known as prison industries and operated by a federal agency called UNICORE.

As we drove, I observed the country-like setting of green grass, small hamlets and barns. What I was viewing was horse farms. I said to the marshals, "Boy, I am here for the Kentucky derby." The derby is the only thing I am aware of about Kentucky, except for the motion picture westerns like the Hatfields and the McCoys. To me, a rural state like Kentucky looks a lot like southwest New Jersey with agricultural farms, and I pointed this out to the marshals also. I was seeing homes, then farms, then a few more homes, and soon we were driving on the outskirts of Lexington with its few homes and buildings. I am from the New York metro area of New Jersey and now it seems as if I was on one of my visits to my homeland in South America with lots of trees, grass, and a few buildings. But this time I was on a long visit and not a two-week vacation.

The marshals started communicating by uttering codes like "ten four" at the end of every conversation. I heard a lot of "ten fours" in a NJ county prison in transit to Kentucky.

The sudden need to start communicating told me we were nearing our destination. We were on a road now with less and less homes, then there was none, and the car made a right turn. All I could see was like a hill with a winding road and it seemed as if we were driving up the moors to a castle on the hill. As we got to the top of the hill, the dome top of a brick building became visible. It was not until later I realized that the prison lay behind the mountain top and it stretched far back and wide than the misleading image it presented at first appearance. The marshal pulled up to the right and radioed in with words like "R&D come in," and I said to myself being an engineer that R&D means Research and Development, but I would soon realize it meant Receiving and Distribution.

To get to R&D, there were two barbed-wire fences separated twelve feet apart with a four-foot-wide walkway between two gates. There were two gates, and when one gate is open the other is closed. No two gates are in the open position at any time. The exterior gate opened electronically and I stepped in with a cane in right hand and my left hand cuffed. The gate behind me closed and I stepped in. When that exterior gate closed behind me and although the other gate was not opened yet, it dawned upon me that I was definitely locked out from the outside world. The inside gate opened and the prison guard met me, and I stepped out of the barbed wire enclosure and I was inside the prison grounds. The guard observed I was not in leg irons like the usual, so when the marshal came in (both gates opened and closed sequentially), he brought my leg irons with the court instructions package.

When prisoners are transferred, all handcuffs and leg irons must be turned over in sets whether on or off the prisoner's body. I was now about to be received and processed in one of the most renowned federal prison hospitals in America, where mobsters, drug addicts, murderers, are all being housed because they have or supposed to have some kind of medical problem and are here temporarily for treatment, some for as long as three years. I would also find out later that many of them had no health problems. They are usually young, busted for drugs, pled guilty and sent here as some kind of reward for pleading guilty. They were rewarded for not being sent to a hard core prison. They were ideal candidates for UNICORE. It was here that the famous Queen of Mean and of real estate spent a few years. That's right, you guess right, our very own from New York, and her name was Leona Helmsley. Even an ex-governor from next door state of Tennessee spent some time here.

A Different World

I was not in Research and Development (R&D), but in Receiving and Distribution. My manacles were removed. Since the R&D officer was processing the previous prisoner, I was instantly put in a holding cell. There were three cells and it was cold in there with nothing to sit on but cold concrete.

The previous person waiting in the cell next door was taken and processing continued. Before I was locked in, I kept asking to make a phone call to my new lawyer or to the family in NJ, but I was told, "Later, in a little while." I would later find out that this right to use the phone was violated. I wanted my family to know where I was, not just a little far away, but all the way down to southeastern United States, more than a thousand miles away. I also found out how the government's practice was to take prisoners as far away from their families in order to make visits a burden to them due to economics.

The steel door was thick. I have never seen such a big key in my life. I said to myself, *"Is this the type of confinement I will be in with just a toilet? How can I sleep in a setting like this with my medical problem? I would die here."* Then my door opened and I was relieved I was leaving this depressing moment, but instead, another arrival was put in storage with me. That's when I first met Al from Memphis, Tennessee. He was very quiet, about forty-four years old. I told him I was hungry although I had eaten a cold sandwich at five that morning in N.J. I told him I needed to make a phone call to let my people know where I was. He said to me, "They will feed you. They have to feed you. What time is it now, twelve, It should be chow time. They should bring us a tray. We should get some food, because chow won't be until five or six." I said to myself *"chow?"*

I once heard that word mentioned in western movies. He asked me if I came from the street. I said no. Later I would find out what "street" and "down" meant. Because of my answer to Al, I was not a regular career criminal for I replied that I did not come from the streets. I asked him what he was in here for and he replied "for evaluation." He was brought in from a maximum security federal prison in Illinois. I thought he said Maryland. I would find out one month later about Marion and what it was meant to be sent there in the first place. Al said he would not speak to the guards at Marion when they talk to him and this was how he was diagnosed as being "out in the head."

There is a unit at the Lexington facility that houses inmates with psychological problems. Al said to me, "He will let you make a phone call, he seems nice," referring to the R&D processor, "there he is, ask him." So I uttered through the small mesh opening above the five-foot level of the wall to let me use the phone and again I was told "later." The door opened again and we were given papers to fill out for information including medical and family history. Later I would find out that I was ruled in as a candidate for psychological detention because I filled all the correct information in the wrong column and I would be observed as being mentally insane. This proved I was disoriented, confused, depressed and disturbed on being in such a foreign and strange surrounding.

I was finally brought out at 2:30 PM, fingerprinted, processed and put back into the cell. About an hour later, I was taken to the last room. This is the last cell-like enclosure before leaving the R&D area. There I met with what I thought was a doctor for evaluation after processing. He said he is a "PA." I asked him what a PA is. I told him I had never heard about a PA before. He said "Physician Assistant." I had one Xanax, a relaxer, that was handed over by the marshal, and the PA said "take this because it would be the last one you will get here. We don't give Xanax here." After reading all the nineteen medications I wrote on the forms, he further stated that I would not get all the medications I was taking before and that some would be dropped, including hypertension and for back pain, and some of my narcotic analgesic medication. I said to myself *"I thought this was a medical facility. How am I going to make it, how am I going to survive?"* I did, but the almighty God had to save me. Al was being processed next, then put back into the cell. During his processing, I was taken to the clothing cell where I took off all my garments except the underwear I was allowed to keep, but not before I spread my behind wide open, my mouth and groin checked. I was put into prison clothes with no pockets. I was given a pair of slippers. I asked about my own clothes and shoes and was told I won't need them and that my belongings would be shipped back home. All identifications are taken from prisoners. I was assigned a number by which each inmate is identified by throughout institution life. I was put back into the holding cell. Al already had the type of clothes I had on. He was not alone, and this was when I first met Reggie from Detroit, Michigan.

At about 5:30 PM, we were each given a bedroll, which includes a blanket, sheet and pillow case. The three of us were taken through more solid doors with large key holes into several walkways then into the main hallway I would come to know as the main corridor. As we were led along, I saw people in wheelchairs, some with one or no legs. I said, "My God, what are these harmless people doing here?" My mind went into shock. Tomorrow I would see a greater infirmity setting I have ever seen. Al was met by another corrections officer and it seemed that he was taken out of the building, but he was taken through a door into another hallway that led to the commonwealth north psychological unit. Reggie and I would not see him for over a month for he was isolated from the rest of the inmate population.

Reggie was met by another CO at the elevator and was taken away to another unit. I was taken on the elevator to the third floor, which is called the health care unit (HCU), known as the hospital unit. I went down a ramp that met with the second level where there are one-man rooms. I was in Room 222. Next door I asked Tom, whom I got to know by name later and with some years to go, about some food, and he said, "You better hurry." I asked him where, and he told me to go back pass the mess hall where I was on my way in before I got on the elevator, so I went up on the elevator.

There were a few inmates in the massive hallway leading to the mess hall. Later I would find out that they had eaten and were in the yard or library or at recreational facilities or on their way back to their units. I walked up to the big glass and wooden door and the CO working that area was just locking the door with people inside working. Some were wearing khaki like me and a few wearing white as if they were in a bakery, but all were prisoners. I knocked on the door and the guard came up and asked, "What do you want?" I replied, "I come for my dinner," then he responded, "Chow is over." I said to him, "But I haven't eaten all day and I just got here." He replied, "You came from the street?" I said no. He continued, "You have never been in a prison before?" and I replied no, then he said "I thought so." He then ordered one of the workers to fix me up something.

The workers were cleaning up before the "move" at seven in the evening. Later I would know what "move" meant. I sat in the dining room alone and ate some stew. I left most of the food. I spent most of the eating time thinking and looking around. The seating was like a burger king setting to hold about one hundred people. Later I would be apprised that there were five dining rooms, nine separate units and several buildings that produced millions in profits for the institution with a population of 1600, including the women prisoners who were just recently separated and given their own building outside our main perimeter.

About 6:50 PM, I returned to my bunker and chatted with Tom, who only gave short answers. It indicated to me that short answers are what you will get from anyone, including the guards, ninety-nine percent of the time unless they are feeling different at that moment. Tom felt at home with family pictures and lots of ordinary things a five-by-eight room can hold, including a cabinet, a chair and a small table. The next day about 2:30 PM, I was told by a guard that I had to leave because single rooms are given out by seniority of the institution occupants. I kept myself from asking any more questions to Tom because his answers were getting shorter. He was about over forty, white and from the Sunshine State and was "down" (convicted) for narcotics.

I took a shower across the hall. I did not know how I would feel if another guy took a shower with me at the same time. At that time of the evening, most people had taken their showers before chow, especially the inmates in the HCU because we were supposed to be the sickest people. At 8:45, I was sleeping. I was up at three waiting to get out. At five, a light was shined upon me, but I was sitting up and wide awake. I had just spent my first night in a federal prison.

Most of the people I have seen in this area are all middle-aged. I went and sat down in a chair in the TV room about 6:30. It was still dark outside and the dead of winter. Some people appeared from their rooms, walked through the TV room and up the ramp, others were coming down the ramp and into their rooms. I asked, "Where are those people coming from?" and was told "from breakfast." I then asked, "When is breakfast?" and he said that breakfast started half an hour ago. He told me to hurry up before breakfast is finished.

I walked up the ramp past the guard at the main entrance to the unit, got on the elevator and went to breakfast. There were several guards at the main entrance to the dining room, then two more guards at the kitchen entrance. I followed the person in front of me and picked up a tray and had my breakfast watched by the guards all the time, which made me very uncomfortable. I went back to my quarters and then one of the two men sitting in the TV room said to me, "You better hurry to the laundry and get your clothes," and I said to myself, *why do I have to go to the laundry, I just got here.* He must have noticed my amazement, so he said, "Those clothes you have on were just temporary, so they could get rid of the ones you came in with. When you go down there, they will give you a set of clothes and shoes."

I was directed to the laundry located at the Level 1 basement, which seemed a dungeon away. After walking through awhile, it seemed like a maze before I got there. I walked away with five pairs of pants, shirts, underwear and socks, a green work-type jacket, cap and a pair of pyjamas. Only two underwear and two socks are replaced every sixty days. As I walked away, I knew I could not wear those boots due to the injury to my legs three and a half years earlier.

It was now eight in the morning and I was sitting in the TV room when a guard came up and said, "Who is Geret?" pronouncing my name wrong with that southern accent. I replied, "I am." Then he said, "You have to go to A&O." I said, "Whah, where?" He only answered to where. He took out his keys, walked to a door, opened it, locked it behind us and we got on the elevator. This was the first and last time I rode the elevator exiting from the lower ramp level of the third floor unit inmate quarters all the way down to the first floor main level. Only corrections officers can ride and exit into inmate quarters when they do not have to or want to walk up and down the ramp. They can control the elevator movement with a special key. I exited into the main corridor, but turned right instead of left to the dining room. Using his directions, I stepped outside the building, through the door, and felt the cold air. I could even see the sky. I walked fifty feet to the end and turned right into the building.

Admissions and Orientation, called A&O, is located on the ground level under the HCU unit. My unit is located three levels under the HCU unit. I would find out and later about the awful truth behind being in the prison system and how the government benefits financially, and how inmates are continuously being subjected to abasement due to UNICORE and prisons as a business.

I finally got to the clinic at one in the afternoon and told them I had not received any medication since five of the previous day. The way one of the nurses dresses reminded us it was Valentine's Day. I was told I must see a doctor first. I told them I did not feel well. Due to my age and previous medications, I was checked for blood pressure, which was 167/103. I was told to go and have chow and the pressure should come down. I was shocked at such a diagnosis and was very afraid for my health and this was my first full day here. After seeing a doctor, I was told to pick up my medication at the pill line. I asked around for the pill line and was told it was on the main lobby.

I went to the pill line at three and was told no medicine was there for me and I should come back later. At about 5:30 PM, I attempted to leave the unit. Men were standing by the doorway of the east and west entrances of the unit quarters, but away from the guard control center and the unit main exit door. I proceeded to go downstairs when the guard said to me, "It is not move yet." I replied, "Not mooo!" for that was what I thought I heard, because of his deep southern accent. I asked someone what the guard was saying, because somehow I felt that I was not supposed to go anywhere at that moment. I was stunned and did not know what to do. All I wanted was to go downstairs for my medicine. Then it was explained to me "you can't leave the unit until the move time," one inmate said to me and I said, "oh." Still not knowing what is "move," I knew that I could not leave at that moment. I never received any medication until 7:30 and they were watered down, even below generic standards and names I have never heard about before. I was afraid to take them. I prayed to God for my survival because I felt I may not make it out of here and may never see my family again. I could feel the tears in my eyes.

I called my wife and attorney to let them know where I was. I tried using my AT&T calling card. I knew the card number by heart, but I was told by one of the guys that direct coin-operated phones were recently taken out. Only collect calls could be made. Two months later my home phone would be disconnected due to my obsolescence to comply. I asked the chaplain if I could use the phone and he said that I had my free call when I came to the prison, and only in the event of death in the family that I would be allowed to use it free again. I told him I was never allowed to make that call I asked for on the first day of my arrival. I realized then at that moment in the chaplain's office that my rights under the law were violated the very first day of my arrival. He did not allow me to make that call.

The Move

I mentioned earlier about my encounter with a guard when attempting to retrieve whatever medicine I could get, especially since I was diagnosed one month earlier by my personal physician of having unstable angina and the likelihood of having a myocardial infarction. This means a fucking heart attack.

Move is a verb and definitely a noun when applied in prison surroundings. It means something is about to begin, or in progress, or something that is ended. In a twenty-four hour day, move is the most important command and control of institutional life in all federal prisons. To go to any part of the facility, whether to the clinic, to meals, to church, to recreation, library, education department, to work (yes, that's right), to bed and anything, everything I might have forgotten to mention. It also means from all of the above destinations. The move command is issued from the monitoring control center within the compound and transmitted through radio that every guard carries on his or her person. The move command allows the institution to account for the inmates' whereabouts without following them around. When the command is announced, elevators that were immobile would start to operate. Inmates can be seen coming out of buildings, in the corridors, hallways, all of them traveling from one destination to another. At the end of the move, which is ten minutes in duration, destination doors are locked with a key by a guard inside or outside that destination. No one can leave a destination until the next move or with the approval of correctional offers. If anyone is caught between the end and beginning of a move in an area he is not supposed to be in without a pass or approval, he could be punished severely.

I was caught up into this a few times in my first few days in this strange world, but was overlooked by the guards because somehow I was viewed by them as being disoriented. I was not only out of it most of the time, and I did not appear to them that I was ever "down" before. As a matter of fact, it was because I was not down before why I was overlooked and more which I will mention later. My behavior was observed for about two weeks and on the third week, I was viewed as to be evaluated to be placed in Al's unit for the mentally disturbed. All inappropriate moves that were observed were reported through radio and well documented, and when an inmate is periodically evaluated he would be told about them. Periodic evaluation is done in order for an inmate to be placed at a lower level of danger from the danger level evaluated at conviction.

The Conviction: An Ill-gotten Plea

O n January 3, 1996, I was convicted in a New Jersey federal district court. The conviction violated the law of exegesis and the court wrongfully sentenced me on a vitiated ill-gotten plea. Moreover, I would find out six months later that the conviction and sentencing judgment was all illegal, causing me to be wrongfully imprisoned that not only destroyed me mentally, emotionally, socially, including my career, family and community, but also my existing overall deteriorating health all at the hands of evil doers of the federal government.

In June of 1992, I suffered a serious accidental injury on federal property. Yes, I worked for the government as a postal clerk in a large mail processing facility in western New Jersey. I was ordered by the supervisor managing a regular Sunday skeleton crew to perform duties outside of my job classification. Two other guys and I lifted a five-by-six-foot, one-inch-thick steel plate and positioned it as a portable ramp at the bay of the loading dock in order to construct an upward bridge to transport 450 pounds postal container with mail. The reason for the ramp adaption was because the truck that brought in the mail broke down twenty-five feet away while reversing into position to deliver the cargo, but the hydraulic lift at the back of the truck worked so each container was lowered to the ground and we pushed them up the ramp. The last container tumbled and I felt a quick hit on my left chin bone. With half an hour to go, the supervisor concentrated on how much processing could be achieved, which included ten minutes to wash up. No attempt was made to find out how serious my injury was.

At home and one and a half hours after the accident, I took my boots off to shower and saw blood in my socks. I examined my leg and it appeared what looked like a skin cut. I washed it with peroxide. The next day at work, I found myself limping. A band aid was applied by the nurse and was put on light duty. On the third day, the nurse who authorized any further medical treatment was out. On the fourth day, the nurse was still out so the superintendent ordered the supervisor to take me to the clinic, which diagnosed that I needed immediate medical treatment right after the accident. It was also diagnosed that the bone had been cut and I needed stitches, but since it had been three days since the accident, it was much too late to do any stitching. One week later, I would be hospitalized due to severe discoloration of the leg and a swollen knee. I would find out then that the accident destroyed the knee and I was facing half a chance of amputation to my lower leg. With three weeks and countless doctors, the leg was saved and the knee was operated on four months later. The accident left me permanently damaged. I would later develop degenerated joint disease and severe muscular skeleton problems of the whole body, and physical therapy for one and a half years did not help. It took six months to make a full 360-degree turn on the crank with no torque on a stationary bicycle. The government paid me seventy percent of my regular salary from which they deducted premiums for my private medical insurance.

I was charged for fraud because I negotiated real estate contracts totaling $18,000 within two and a half years since the accident. The government and the whole facility where I worked knew I was licensed in real estate. I negotiated contracts for some of its employees before the accident and after the accident. Through discovery, the government (management) admitted they knew of my periodic real estate affiliations and did nothing about it, but waited long enough and sent undercover agents posing as buyers who called me. On that day of the phone call, I was in pain for I had just returned from aquatic therapy. I was under surveillance for several weeks, they were observing my movements, and they knew that I would sometimes stop at the real estate office on my way home from therapy. I would hang around not more than an hour and would answer the phone, hoping that the call would be for my house which was on sale by the office because I was facing foreclosure. By observing my movements, the agents knew about when to call the office. I answered the phone and they were looking for a house that fit the description of mine. Management at the postal service had an obligation to inform me if I was doing any wrong. I was facing foreclosure and my house was on the market. I was glad to find a buyer. Because I showed my house and along with two other public listings. I was entrapped through audio-visual surveillance.

I was assigned a public defender who coerced me to plea guilty and on May 11, 1995. My reluctant plea of guilt was entered by my public defender. I would later discover the plea was planned and carried out. With a zero criminal history, I was sentenced on January 3, 1996 to twelve months in a federal prison, which shocked me, my family, friends and associates, the medical community, the legal community and the Federal Bureau of Prisons officials due to the degree and nature of the offense. Something had been terribly gone wrong and a terrible injustice had been done to me. After a total of six months of incarceration and two years of prosecutorial dilemma, I discovered I was dealing with persecutors and evil doers doing what they were supposed to do, that was being agents to their evil empire.

Surviving in My New Home

As mentioned before, I was moved from the one-man room and put in the dormitory. I attended A&O, which explained about the institution requirements. The clinic told me I had a multitude of problems, but assured me they would try to accommodate me. I asked them to contact my doctors back home for my immediate medical history information so I could be properly treated, but they said they could not. I asked why, and was told that I myself had to contact my doctors to send them the information. My attorney sent them the information and I had copies also. Because the medications were changed and the food was different, no sleep, and the sight of so many sick people in wheelchairs without legs and arms, I began to lose weight, my pains increased and I became a walking time bomb. Albert in a wheelchair, a somewhat religious man in his sixties, advised me to "come to church." After five days, on February 18, I slept one and a half hours only. Maybe the prayer meeting service at seven in the evening that Sunday night helped me.

I continued to get neck, chest and back pains, because they stopped giving me Percocet after the first three days from issue. I tightened my back brace hoping it would help my back. On February 25, 1996, I had my first chronic attack at the institution. Chronic attacks were well documented by my New Jersey physicians. The guard called the PA on Sunday duty and reported my illness. He returned and told me to take a dose of all my medications and "that should do it." I was shocked at such a diagnosis. I went to the clinic on Monday at sick call and saw the physician in charge. He told me to come back at 7:30 that morning and see a PA. As she was checking my blood pressure, I said to her that it was too high because I was not getting my proper blood medication. She knew I understood the gauge so she could not lie to me. I also told them that I want my narcotic analgesic medication for my severe leg and back pain. I was told to pick up my prescription at the pill line at seven, but there was none. Not till my next attack a few weeks later that I would get some medical attention. I had some Methocarbamol for muscle relaxer at my first issue for thirty days. It helped a little.

On February 27, my blood pressure was checked and it was even higher. I was told I complained too much, and there would be no more Methocarbamol, so when it runs out in a few days, I should not expect any because the institution is about to discontinue it. I told her I had not been sleeping, and she replied that I had been assigned to see the psychiatrist for my sleep disorder. I felt to the point I would fall down, and since February 13, I slept only six and a half hours. I had my appointment with the psychiatrist and as I mentioned earlier, he told me that I seemed suicidal, especially since I indicated suicidal information on the papers at R&D at first entry, and also because I was on the drug Lorazepam. I told him I had those pills at the pill line over two weeks ago and only for three days. I also told him that I entered the correct information in the wrong column at R&D. No way I was going to let this guy send me to the crazy ward. He went on by saying that the staff was considering putting me in the psychological unit and his job was to certify my transfer. Anyhow, it did not happen, thank god. Then I read a magazine that was sitting on one of the tables in the TV lounge on the west side.

I could always be seen walking and limping with my cane ambulating painfully from the east to the west wing. The magazine described acceptance and denial steps of inmates in prison. Somehow, I accepted only my immediate state of being and not the reason I was sent there in the first place. I slept three hours that night and felt fresh the next day. I had to accept with reluctance that no matter how shock I am, I will only be given as much help as the facility wanted to give. In the January 3, 1997 issue of The Star-Ledger Newark newspaper, a spokesperson for the Federal Bureau of Prisons in Washington made reference that "the facility specializes in the care of patients with chronic medical problems." The Newark police chief was being sent there on a conviction. My internist from NJ specifically wrote the trial court (there was no trial in my case), which was hell bent to send me to prison on a misdemeanor charge. The physician wrote:

"The defendant's condition appears to be chronic and is associated with flares of acute attacks requiring steroids, Allopurinol, Motrin and narcotic analgesics to abate and control the pain. He has had episodes of unpredictable chest pain precipitated by stress and associated with liable hypertension. He has been taking medication for this condition consisting of Procardia, Tenormin, and Xanax. However, to date, I have no information which would exclude the possibility of coronary disease. If he indeed does have unstable angina, this would place him in high risk for subsequent myocardial infarction. He needs further diagnostic studies to rule out this possibility. Therefore, I still consider his medical condition to be extraordinary and the additional stress anxiety of incarceration could adversely affect his health status."

The rheumatologist also wrote the magistrate: "The defendant has been under my care since July1995. In his condition, he is prone to develop severe episodes of inflammation and pain in multiple joints. The attacks can be quite painful. During these attacks, he will require prompt medical attention."

My urologist also wrote: "The defendant was seen and evaluated for his annual prostate check. His American Urologic Association symptom score is noted to be 35 indicative of severe outlet obstruction secondary to benign prostatic hyperplasia. He has had progressive symptoms of urinary prostate enlargement and outlet obstruction symptoms over the last five-year period and has been followed accordingly through my office. Pharmacologic manipulation in the past has really been unsuccessful and his only alternative other than watchful waiting is prostatic surgery."

My medical condition was disregarded by the court and I surely suffered for it.

I could not get in touch at home. The phone will not accept my calls, so on March 1st I asked the chaplain to use his phone, but as I mentioned earlier, that request is only granted in the case of death. He told me I had my free phone call when I came in. I told him no. As I mentioned earlier, this was when I knew my rights were violated.

On March 4th, I was called to the clinic and was confronted with a horrible discovery which made me feel that I would surely die, for at least once a week at the facility an inmate dies. I was told that the results from the skin test of February 14, 1997 came out positive and that I had tuberculosis. I was shocked. I was also told I must take thirteen pills a week, which they have plenty of in my opinion. Three pills are given at the pill line and you are checked off when given. This is done twice a week. You must also take a once-a-day pill from a thirty-day supply in your possession at any time of the day to offset the liver damage positively consistent with those TB pills. If you do not show up at the pill line, the guards will hunt you down and even throw you into confinement called the hole. They said it was for everybody's safety to take the pills, which I agree to, if it is true that you have TB. But the facility has appropriated a lot of money for this, thus conforming to its physical purpose as a medical prison, but is overshadowed by a much larger and lucrative purpose for its physical existence, which I will discuss in the next chapter. I continued to have severe leg and back problems but with no narcotic analgesic medication.

On March 5th, about 3:57 PM, I was told by the guard to go down to food service so that I could be counted with the afternoon shift workers. I did not even get there in time. From my quarters on the third floor to the mess hall it is about two blocks walking length. All the corridors were clear so I was the lone person getting off the elevator limping with my silver cane towards food service being observed by the main corridor guards, who were radioed that I was coming through because this was an unauthorized move. I proceeded. I think I was the only inmate with a silver cane. All others were made of wood. As I walked I asked myself why the hell I have to leave my bedside to come down here to be counted. This was a psychological way to tell an inmate that he is being assigned to work. On Friday the 8th, I saw my assigned physician for the first time and I told her my name was on the call out list to work in food service. I told her I could hardly walk and I have not worn those shoe boots given to me at the laundry on February 14th, because my feet could not carry them. She immediately gave me a move clearance and sent me to the laundry for a shoe, but I still could not wear them. I asked her why I am being put to work when I have a musculoskeleton problem. She then told me she was told to put me to work and it was out of her hands. Later, she would tell me after she became more acquainted of the seriousness of my health that the clinical director ordered her to put me to work.

As time went on, I found out there was a work committee panel, which maintains a liaison with the medical department and its purpose is to get as much inmates shortly after arrival to be assigned on the work roll, so a strict and consistent labor force is always available in order to maintain their objective of profitability. One day in June, I was sitting next to a black young yesterday's arrival who had been down, about nineteen years, and told me he was already assigned to work in the kitchen where he worked at the prison he was just brought from. I can imagine a warden of one prison calling up another for some workers to upkeep his appropriations of funds.

My physician then assigned me to a sanitary position, meaning a sitting position. On Sunday, March 10th, I was on the list to be at food service at ten in the morning for the count. I had just returned from church at 9:57. So again I had to struggle down there. The food service supervisor speaking to an inmate (who seemed on good terms together) said that "they must be looking for trouble, sending a guy like that down here." He observed the rubber at the base of my cane that could make me fall if the floor is wet, which happened often because of spills, so he let me sit and put napkins in holders. I ate my lunch and went back upstairs at 11:30 AM. I never signed any employment papers for my forty-four cents, four-hour-a-day job, because I considered it an insult and degrading thing they were doing to the inmates.

On Monday, 11th, I was told to report to food service at eight though my name was not on the call out list at the guard's desk. Call out lists are made up by eight in the evening of the previous day; the guard told me he was called from F/S for me to come down and I was not about to argue with the guard. There was another guard-supervisor in charge, so he instructed me to mop the mess hall since breakfast had been over. I told him I could not do that. He then told me to pick up the trays from some of the tables, and again I said I could not do that. He could clearly see I was wearing rubber slippers, back brace, and a cane for ambulation. He then said, "How about wiping the tables?" I told him I would try with my left hand knowing full well that tables with trays had to be picked up by one of the other guys. The other guys were all black and young, so we became acquainted, observing me as a father figure because they all could have been my sons. They confided in me about their misfortunes and none of that group had any medical problems. But because I was a part of their labor force group, they called me "pops."

My assignments would come to an abrupt end for it lasted not more than eleven days, because on March 25th, I suffered a massive chronic attack. Yesterday they had me giving out bacon in the kitchen because it was country breakfast for lunch. My legs hurt real bad that night. Now I could not move. The guard was called and I was subsequently put in a wheelchair, given crutches so I could get in the bathroom for the three steps to the toilet from the bathroom door. I remained in the wheelchair to the day I left, July 10, 1996. Attempts were made for me to still work from the wheelchair, but the excuses were that my name was still on the work committee list or that food service never received any convalescence papers making me ineligible to work. Convalescence meant that one is temporarily not able to work until recovery. This meant that they intended to keep me on work status, which I could not understand except for what the physician told me confidentially. It seemed to me that because I was hurt working for the government that got me in this mess in the first place, being on work status could be used to dispute any future law suit compensation claims and to use prison work records to support their argument. This is another example of the government's evil doings against its citizens.

On Friday, May 10, 1996, I suffered a heart attack about one in the afternoon, and nitroglycerin was administered. A jar of the medication was given to me to keep on my person twenty-four hours a day. That same evening while I lay on my bed, inmate Andrea Sympson died of a massive heart attack while looking at the Holyfield fight in the east wing TV room. It scared the hell out of me when I was informed till next morning. I remember hearing of Sympson's constant fight to be allowed to go outside to get a heart transplant, but the warden would not allow it. His fight led to media attention, which was broadcasted on the afternoon of Friday, March 15, 1996, but somehow most of us missed it.

Many of us hurried back from supper, which started late that day, and it meant we were late getting back to see the 5:30 news. But not all inmates from my unit went for grub and they saw it. I remember returning from supper and sitting right behind Sympson in the TV room waiting hopelessly for his segment to come on. The warden walked by and then said to us, "You guys missed it," or words to that effect. This was a clear admittance that it was an intentional act on the prison's part to deny us the opportunity to see the segment. Supper was intentionally started later so we would miss the 5:30 PM news from the TV view room upstairs. The warden had to take the elevator to come upstairs just so that he could see our disappointment for he knew we would be sitting in the TV room waiting for the segment that already passed.

After the tragedy, on the next day, Mother's Day, I had chest pain symptoms that started in church and worsened at 10:25 AM, by which time I was back at my bunk. At 10:35, I was rushed upstairs to the prison hospital and nitro, which I had already taken in church, was given to me by a physician assistant. I was taken twice outside to the university hospital in downtown Lexington because my own prison physician said to me that she had no answers about my symptoms, and that they were complex. So I was first taken out on May 29, 1996 to see a rheumatologist, who recommended the same uric acid medications I was taking. I told him that he should take a bone scan for I had not any since May of '95, and that my NJ physician did a yearly scan to monitor my musculoskeleton diagnostic problems that developed from the outcome of the accident. He then informed that if the prison instructed him he would have done so.

Back at the prison, blood test showed my uric acid was low. I saw my physician again because my pains in my feet and back worsened and I was still in the wheelchair. She continued to say she still could not understand how I continued to get these attacks with a uric acid as low as 4.5, but my NJ physician explained why; that was after I left Kentucky. My physician at the prison was able to convince her boss, the clinical director (who was adamant against too real costly treatment like Sympson needed),that I needed a bone scan, which the prison hospital are not equipped to do, likewise many other medical procedures, despite of the wide misconception on how they are specialized with inmates' chronic problems. The contracted U.K. hospital is where it is really done. So I was taken back on Friday, June 21, 1996 for my bone scan.

Two and a half days went by and I was never put on the call out to discuss the results and treatment from that bone scan. On July 31, 1996 and back in New Jersey, my physician contacted the university hospital in Kentucky and the shocking results were faxed to my rheumatologist. The diagnosis was that I had severe joint disease and a collapsed arch in my foot. I was very hurt at this disclosure. I knew something was terribly wrong. I was first sent to a place on an illegal conviction. On top of that, my health was terribly endangered just like Sympson, who was also Afro-American. We have been maligned and demagogued by the evil powers of the American criminal justice system.

So I carried my nitro twenty-four hours, my severe bone disease, my aches and pains to the day I left the facility in July 10. But my infirmities under the bureau of prisons would not end there. It would go on another three weeks, incarcerated at county prisons not equipped for any kind of infirmity, but maximum security under inhumane conditions, including cold and filthy preparations. I was processed six times at six detention centers, taken across to America's heartland before I was finally returned to my home state and freed all due to the vindictiveness, intentional infliction to cause harm and emotional distress by the prosecution and the evil empire of the law enforcement division of the government.

The Truth Inside the Walls

As of February 29, 1996, documentation indicated that there were 128 prisons and with a population of 102,201 inmates in the federal prison system.

According to a news report on August 19, 1997, at exactly 6:50 AM on W.C. B.S radio, America has the largest percent of its population in prisons than any other country in the civilized world. This was quoted by Charles Osgood. Naturally, this includes both state and federal prison populations.

The Federal Bureau of Prisons is supposed to be about correction, but the larger picture is hidden from the public. It is also a conglomerate of industrial might with lucrative returns at the mercy of its prisoners. A separate agency known as UNICORE oversees and manages what is commonly called prison industries. People outside the prison world have been fed one thing, that is, prisoners do odd jobs like cleaning and cooking, which is good for them because it relieves their mental stress of incarceration. If you remember before, I had mentioned on my visit that as I approached the top of the hill in Lexington Kentucky, I found how obscured the medical center is viewed from a distance. It is stretched beyond many acres of buildings that do not house inmates. These buildings are its large industrial complex just as a private corporation. But the public is told different.

In the January 13, 1997 issue of the Newark Star-Ledger, there were quotations made by Federal Bureau of Prisons spokesman Bill Bechtold in Washington in the profile of recently convicted Newark police chief, who was sent to Lexington, that "the facility is located seven miles north of Lexington and is surrounded by herds of cattle and tobacco farms and that the facility specializes in the care of patients with chronic medical problems." I did not see any cattle unless I needed a telescope. I did see a horse or two as far as the eyes could see. I know about cattle because I originated from an agricultural society. What we, the American government, talk about human rights violation around the world, especially in Asia and South America, is happening right here.

Recently, horrifying disclosures were made about Chinese immigrants in New York Chinatown, when it was investigated by a local New York TV station following up by the Department of Labor, but the news soon trickled down and we heard nothing more about it, not that I can remember and I follow the news constantly. Working in UNICORE also established status between the inmate workers, who are predominantly white, and the food service and cleaning workers who are predominantly black and Hispanics. About fifty percent of the inmates are not inmates with chronic health problems. This issue is well documented for in that same Washington spokesman's statement of January 13, 1997, it indicated "while many of the inmates at the center have medical problems," Bechtold noted that "a number of prisoners are healthy and assigned to the general population, where they are responsible for duties in the kitchen and laundry room."

The terrible irony behind that statement clearly states that if those inmates did not have medical problems, then why in hell they are there. I will tell you why. They were sent there to work in the kitchen, laundry and beyond. The sentences for most of them who are predominant black and Hispanics are mostly drug related and as much as ten to twenty years. Many of these minorities are young and under twenty-five years old. There was this guy I met in the library who just turned twenty-one. He seemed so young and healthy. He told me he was in for drugs, finished three and has eleven years to go, but he finally got in to work at UNICORE after his menial eleven-cent-per-hour year-long job. That's right, they made it a contest to get into UNICORE. Yes sir, no sir, good behavior, church attender (especially perceived as a black disciplined trait) working long hours, doing anything and everything right, and yes, still be on the waiting list, which is about 210 ahead of you because UNICORE pays a little more than eleven cents and enough to purchase tennis rocket and shorts, snacks, and real food from the commissary that you can cook in microwaves located in each unit. You could buy branded cigarettes instead of the tasteless cheaper kind you have never heard of before. Many inmates are levied court assessment fees and fines that must be paid before release. At $5.00 a month for some jobs, and with no family support, if an inmate has a large fine or restitution, he could kiss the streets goodbye.

For these young men, through their guilty pleas and promises to their mothers that they would be sent to a nice place, these became baits and these young bucks were subjected to slave labor at the mercy of the federal government for ten, fifteen, twenty years of their life at prisons around the country. Many of them have produced lost generations due to the non-productive use of their genes. Other prisons manufacture furniture, clothing, blankets, shoes, and many other products, and sell them at market prices. Prison is big business. This statement was affirmed by a visiting chaplain.

One day in the afternoon, I was sitting in my wheelchair in the TV room on the west side when he came by and started chatting with some of the guys sitting at another table. I remember seeing him talk to inmates at different locations in my unit. He dressed in regular street casual clothes just like volunteers that visit the facility. He was a volunteer and not paid by the prison as the other chaplains. He walked over to my table and I asked him who he was for I had seen him before. He explained. He went on to state that when he was late in his adolescent years, he got in trouble and was sent to prison for nine months. His life changed since. He tried to give us solace as to our physical existence. I pointed out to him that after being there a few weeks, I came to the conclusion that this place was operating like a business because of what I had observed. He responded, "This is a business." I was shocked at such an admission that it was true. Because prison is big business, there is a continuity of supply and demand; therefore, people must be found guilty convicted, and given long sentences in order to fulfill the requirements of the evil system.

The items the inmates purchase come from the commissary; this too is big business. The commissary also carry cologne, aspirin (this is a medical center), prepared dinners, lots of canned products and haberdasheries, so inmates who want a snack better continue to work at slave pay. Many times I have seen inmates ask another for some cookies or crackers in the evening because of hunger for he could not eat what was prepared for dinner. The inmate would then promise that when he goes to the commissary he would return the favor. Now this inmate either could not work and was depending on family to send some money, or he would be receiving his menial pay of a couple dollars, which, by the way, does not get in your hands for any money coming to you from inside or outside goes right into your commissary account. You can see inmates checking what looked like an ATM machine that displayed how much money is left in his account. This machine is located at the main corridor.

There had been reports that the commissaries has had past U.S. presidents as its co-owners. I guess commissaries is a privilege and since the inmates have long prison sentences, this setting is supposed to keep them comfortable; there were about 600 prison guards also called correction officers and hacks. Hack is a word I never understood maybe because I never have enquired enough about, but was used by the more seasoned and experienced prisoners, and oh, yes, they are also called cops and police. Ron said to me that anyone that carries keys is a hack. As a matter of fact, there are two sets of people in a prison; there are the hacks and the convicts. He said the doctor, nurse, librarian, kitchen supervisor, laundry personnel, education department training personnel, the guards that maintain order in the units, the case workers, counselors and, yes, the chaplain are the hacks. Though they don't carry guns, he went on to say that they all have to go out periodically to the firing range (located on those same thirty-seven acres) and practice in case there is an uprising. I asked him, "the priest, too," me being a Roman Catholic; "everybody," he replied. Side arms can be seen only when an inmate with a higher level of public danger was being taken outside the prison for special medical treatment not available at the prison, or if he was being transferred. By having keys, each of the above mentioned personnel could secure any area he or she is in at any time for any reason. Inmates could be immediately secured in any area even in the recreation yard, which has a main entrance and exit, and there were occasions when they had to tough out down pour of rain or developing snow fall until the emergency lockdown is over. This action is like sheep or cattle herded in a particular area.

Then there is the educational system. Some people do receive a high school diploma and that is good, but everyone must go to school, that is if your pre-sentence report indicated none at sentencing. There were many people well matriculated that were forced to go to attend classes although they were lawyers, teachers and doctors just because their high school diplomas were not mentioned in their pre-sentence reports, but their B.S. and P.H.D were mentioned. An eighty-two-year-old New York doctor, whose bunk was next to Ronnie, was forced to attend school until he got a medical waiver from his prison doctor that at that time he could not attend, but as far as I know, he was still on the school list the day I left. My pre-sentence report indicated I had my G.E.D, my A.A.S and my B.S.

I guess the doctor's pre-sentence report indicated M.D., which was not enough. We could not believe our ears. Another guy from Minnesota who was in the military when he got his high school diploma which was sent to him, but prison officials would not accept it. It was vivid proof he had a diploma. The truth is that the prison has appropriated funds by the government for the high school diploma programs for each prisoner. For each inmate that attends school, the institution gets $2,500.00, and each inmate has two chances making the appropriation go up to $5,000.00, so the more attendances and failures, the more the money. Some inmates never got pass the fourth grade, but their signatures are there on record for attendance. Some of them really wanted to succeed, but their obsolescence of earlier educational years deprived them the chance, and the prison is where the instructors are viewed as kindergarten teachers. There were those who had their diplomas sent from their still functional high school, but although this stopped them from further attending any more classes, their signatures had already guaranteed the full appropriation.

From my observation, the appropriation for medical service is at the top of the list. This is supposed to be a medical facility. I had mentioned in the previous chapter about my T.B. diagnosis. The thirteen pills a week is vigorously enforced. You had to take them for six months. The institution was never out of them. The sad thing was, some people never really had it and forced to take something that endangered their lives. After about four months, I spoke with an inmate at the pill line. I knew him from the dining room where he had been working for several months. He had been down for a few years. I asked him why he was at the pill line every day. He said that taking three T.B. pills all at once twice a week was too dangerous, so he asked to take one daily. He said he told them their diagnosis was wrong because people originating from British protectorate countries were once inoculated for T.B. and any skin test would come up positive. I confronted the clinic about this information. They admitted that the information is true. I told them that I have lived a clean lifestyle and is most unlikely that I contracted anything, and that I was taking something that could damage my liver because it clearly stated that the I.N.H medication is consistent with liver damage. The clinic said to me that they would not stop giving me the medication because they were not taking any chances, although they knew that I originally was from a former British colony and that I had the vaccination, but again the idea of stopping would only be a minus to the appropriation.

I involuntarily continued to take a life-threatening medication, which had to be taken for exactly six months because if a person had T.B. and stopped taking the medication, then he can surely die. I took the medication for four months because I left Lexington on a release order, but vindictively I was kept in the federal system for three more weeks at different holding centers and no T.B. medication was given to me. It was quite obvious that I had to take it before I left, but not after. But as I have often said in my story, God had always been with me or I would have never made it back home.

About Us

The infirmities at Lexington were a disgusting and frightening sight. Never have I seen so many people in wheelchairs at a glance. Once in a while in my life, I would see someone at a hospital or outside a nursing home. I have seen on a few occasions of motorized wheelchairs going down the street, but to see forty or fifty at once troubled me. Some had four limbs, but two limbs are immobile, like the New York twenty-nine-year-old black inmate who could never stand, and at times if he wanted to change his comfort position, he would pick up a leg grabbing it by the knee attempting to take it off the foot rest when the leg and the whole body would shake terribly for about five minutes. He was located in a two-man room on the west side, which had the adaptation for the severely handicapped. We called him New York as a nick name.

That year in 1996, Kentucky beat New York for the basketball championship and we all saw it on TV. The warden allowed that the 10 p.m. count be delayed so everyone, including the guards (many of them Kentuckians), could see the game without interruption. New York told me he was convicted around 1989, serving ten years and had MS in his first year. Compassionate release is given to certain individuals with severe medical problems. In the opinion of many, he and many others deserve compassionate releases, but were never considered. Others like Baker, who was white and from PA, and his family knew a certain congressman, as we were told. Baker, who was also a Marine, got himself into fights with other inmates and guards, placed into the hole (segregation), and moved around by prison officials within the unit because of his bad behavior to comply. Had it been someone else (black), he would have been moved and placed in one of the other less fortunate, unfavorable units. He was finally placed into my area where he could not misbehave because of some of the people were blacks. Anyhow, Baker was told by social services that he would be receiving social security for himself and all his children and how much, all just after his compassionate release. We were shocked he received such precise information about his benefits.

Then there were the three-limb men. I remember one guy coming in one month before I left. He could not ambulate his wheelchair with one hand. His other hand was placed on a separate hand rest. He could not move that hand at all. Inmate companions (I.C.P) are assigned to them in order to help them go to the bathroom and to take a shower. Once, I myself needed help to get in the shower due to my unfortunate chronic attack. I myself was a kind of three-limb and a two-limb inmate when the attack worsened. Inmate companions are usually healthy inmates, most of them very young and from other units less facilitated than the health care unit (HCU). Doing this kind of work gives them a positive image. Helping the sick and the old looks good for their record, especially when it is time for their periodic reviews, because they all want to go to a camp and serve out their sentence.

There is a fourth level with walk-up stairs located on both east and west wing of the third floor health care unit. Some of these inmate companions get the opportunity to be transferred to the HCU and placed in the upper level. This allows them to be readily available to help a fellow inmate. Although this is supposed to be a medical facility, medical attention is not available most of the time, especially in the evening. Inmate companions serve a special purpose in getting any kind of help that may be available under the circumstances. Some of them get paid and when considering the appropriation for private care, eleven cents an hour would never cut it. Older I.C.P do it out of just wanting to help another human being.

Then there are the two-limb men. One bald white southerner, about thirty-eight, with both legs cut off just below the knees, was an efficient pool player and good at ambulating the wheelchair. Then one day I saw him standing. He had put on his artificial leg, but walked so funny that could scare a kid looking at a science fiction movie. I never saw him in those legs again. He played cards a lot. Some said he ran the game, if you know what I mean. In June, there was a two-limb guy brought in for eleven days only so that the government could satisfy the requirements that he was sent to a medical facility after he spent three months in a filthy county jail. He was Italian from the Kentucky-Ohio border. He was placed in the dormitory. He had no lower limbs. He hopped from the bed to the wheelchair. I remember giving him twice some coffee from my locker. We had a hot water kettle.

At mealtime on my second day at the facility, the wheelchairs were assembled at the unit entrance all the way down to the TV room on the west side and to the coin machines forty feet away into the east side—my side. I must have counted forty wheelchairs, and not everyone would go to meals at any time, so you can imagine how many more chairs there were. I said to myself that how could all these poor people be criminals and how could they commit a crime in a wheelchair. I found out later that they were either lookout men or actually had the stuff, selling it. Who would think or even suspect that a poor looking guy sitting on the porch had the white or green stuff. Just show him the money, I guess, then you know. Yes, they are criminals and are probably better off in here because of the constant attention for care from family members like shopping, cleaning, cooking and taking them to the doctor, all may not be endurable for too long.

One guy about forty-five and from North Carolina acts like a redneck and talks rebellious, though I found by talking to him that he could be nice at times. He would get real mad if he could not see his program on in the TV viewing room. He has four limbs, but his feet had no life. He prides himself with his long beard and pony tail, which he takes considerable amount of time to comb and form while looking at the TV from his favorite viewing spot, which if occupied would reflect a quiet rage. I have a habit of trying to talk to people who have been criticized negatively by consensus. I would pick the moment I thought was right. One day, I was in his viewing room on the west side when I asked him about his conviction. He said to me, "You don't belong here but I do." He started stroking his beard, "I deserved to be locked up," he continued. When asked how long, "sixty-five years"; "for what?" I said, "for drugs" he replied. To myself I said he may not last thirty. How can a man be sentenced to sixty-five years for drugs? That is more than for murder. He did not cause anyone's death, at least not through his conviction.

Then there are some inmates in the actual hospital upstairs, which itself is the fourth level of the building main structure, and the elevator goes up there. Above that is the fifth level where I believe the morgue is. These inmates in the hospital never leave for meals. They can be seen once in a while being brought down to the clinic or being rolled outside for some air, but some of them could not even stand to see sunlight and asked to be taken back inside where they are locked in their rooms. They never go to the cafeteria. Their meals are brought to them. Sometimes, an inmate that goes to the hospital is never seen again. I remember a few but won't state their names; there was a southern black man about seventy and about 200 pounds who came in the last day of February before count time. He was brought to the dorm, but he could hardly walk, taking five minutes to go about ten feet. The next day he was put in the hospital. We wondered for a month what happened to him. Speculations were that he died, then shortly thereafter he was brought down and placed in the four-man room off the walkway, which was the last room before the dormitory area.

There was also the chief, a black guy from Africa, who was always sitting by the east side vending area occupied with tables. He could be seen writing letters while cooking in the microwave every day. Some said he had to write every day to his tribe because they were so many. He was taken to the hospital, but never made it alive after a few weeks. No one else I actually knew had returned, at least not to the day that I left. Many others use a walking cane and there were others who walked with disfigured limbs. All the others had problems that could not be viewed just by mere ambulation. There was from the lower level an over eighty-year-old man, who I believed had very poor vision, but was forced to work in the kitchen, I was told. From New Hampshire, a middle-aged white male on a white collar conviction walked with a cane, but swings out one leg and jerks before the leg came down to complete the move. He always had a hard time to carry his tray of food to the table in the dining room. I have seen him drop his tray. I spoke and ate with him many times in the diet dining room. From the dorm, I was the only one that ate in the diet room. There was Don, who came in shortly before I left. The guy from NH was a very intelligent man with a distorted speech that signaled he must have had a stroke. He read a lot. His quarters were a six-man room about twenty-five feet down the hallway before reaching the dormitory, so I saw him all the time on my way in or out.

In the same room, there was a rumor a guy died of TB three months before I left. This is just an excerpt from a larger picture about the infirmities at Lexington. First shocked, then afraid, then sad, then sick when I first saw the state of these human beings I had never seen before; there was a handicapped mechanism in the chapel for wheelchair worshippers. We would be placed in the electric lift and lowered onto the ground. The average wheelchair worshippers were about ten.

As I said earlier, the second day at Lexington I was moved from the one-man room and placed in the dormitory on the east side. The dormitory is where all new arrivals are placed unless an inmate is a paraplegic or he had to be placed in an area considered accessible to the hospital upstairs. There was one empty bed along the left wall and two empty beds in between the nine beds on the opposite side, where the window area is. I chose the bed against the wall. I was the only black inmate and I felt that at the middle position against the wall, I could see everybody at all points including those entering the dormitory. They introduced themselves to me. Halbert to the left of me and the third bunk was first. He was always the first to introduced himself to somebody new and in five minutes he would ask what you were in for, how long is your sentence, and if you came from the streets or from another prison. I told him I came from the county jail in New Jersey, but really I came from the street. When an inmate is not from the street, he somehow is supposed to belong in a place like this, the big house.

Halbert was doing, I think, was ten months on illegal drug charges. He owned a pool hall and bar in Las Vegas. He told me that the famous Las Vegas mod enforcer Tony "The Ant" Spilotro visited his premises and shot some pool. Spilotro's body was found in an Indiana corn field. Some said he was beaten and buried alive according to the book written by F.B.I. agent Bill Romer.

Across the ten-foot pathway of the thirty-by-approximately-seventy-foot dormitory were six guys, one to the far left wall by the window and uses a wheelchair all the time. He preferred to be on the east side though he qualified for the west side with handicap facility. He did go there to shower. His name was Joe. He spoke of anarchy, white superiority, his motorcycle gangs, his rebellious ways and days and racisms, but he could be as ordinary at times. Funny how it never bothered me. The concept was that because my wife was white, it was okay to speak about racial overtones in front of me. Halbert pointed this out at one of our once-in-a-while chat; some of the other good old boys stop by on a visit mostly after supper or on weekends.

Then there was who we called the doctor from New York, who I mentioned before about his high school diploma. Ron was always saying that the doc did not belong here. He always seemed complacent, leaving his bunk just about count time, which is a serious violation. Talking during the count is also a violation and the doc may continue conversing as count is in progress. According to Ron, at age eighty-two, the doc does things at his own schedule and does not understand the realities of prison confinement. He was always getting into conflict with prison officials everywhere in the facility. One time he was lost. He could not find his way out of the dining area. I had noticed him while I was at food service doing the napkins that he was walking back and forth at the inside hallway that separated the dining rooms from the kitchen and tray disposal area. He was led out although it was not move time.

Next to the doctor was Ron, then Pat from Connecticut, Tommy from PA, and Lou from the New York area, and on my right against my wall was the leader of the group, the dorm, the unit, known by almost everyone, his name in books, movies, and television criminal mafia documentaries. He was described in the book "The Enforcer" as once the driver of Al Capone. He was also described in the books as the successor to Capone because of his shrewd, subtle, and obnoxious behavior. He was Chicago under boss, and the boss. His name is Jackie Cerone.

A couple of weeks later after I had arrived, I read "The Enforcer." I felt chilled when Romer said in the book "he killed and killed hundreds." I said, *My god, this man is sleeping ten feet away from me.* Supposed I said something he did not like, my throat may be cut by him or any of the other three mafia guys. Cerone was an octogenarian about eighty-one-and-a-half years old. He was a quiet man but could become enraged at an instant. No one dared get him mad, not even the guards. I remember telling a young white guard (about twenty-six years old and who I chat with once in a while whenever he worked the unit) a month before I left about who that man was that got ill and was taken upstairs to the hospital when he had called the PA. He said he knew Cerone by name whenever he worked the unit, but never knew he was a legendary crime boss. He came by my bunk later and asked me for the name of the book, which he intended to get the next day in town, so he could read about Jackie Cerone. Since he was off, he had read most of the book.

Cerone, Giancana, Arcado and Aiuppa ruled the mafia infiltrations in Las Vegas since the 1950s. Names like Lefty Rosental and Spilotro The Enforcer are some of the few mentioned. In the third month of June 1997 when I was back at home, all their names and faces appeared on A&E TV's special about the mob and Vegas. As a matter of fact, I saw the movie "Casino" in January of 1996 one month before leaving for Kentucky, and Don Rickles played Cerone, a small man, bald head and a health freak, running around the block, walking, exercising just like Bill Romer said, and Cerone tried to continue doing the same in the yard at Lexington, though he had past eighty. He would always offer you something, but don't refuse it.

Even though you do not want it. This made him mad. He would say out loud, "Eat it, it is good for you." You better take it, he would open his eyes wide to scare the hell out of you, reminding you who he was and may still be.

He played cards all night at some location in the building, though the rule was no one should be out of their quarters after twelve midnight, but the guards leave him alone. He slept to when he wanted to and no one dared woke him up, although all beds should be made up by 7:30 AM, even if you are lying on top of the made up bed. He only got up if he had to for his own reasons. Cerone found out in April, two months after I arrived, that he would be paroled in July of that same year. When I was reading the "Enforcer," I would cautiously ask him who Aiuppa was, Giancana, and at times, the other names like "Glick," and he would reply "Oh, him!" and smiled. One of the worst things you could do was to press him for an answer. He did say Lefty, the bastard, was alive and living well. A few weeks later he said to me, "You know that guy, that guy that wrote that book, he is fucking dead, dead of cancer, the lying bastard."

Lou at the other end of the room from Joe was a quiet man. His bed was at the very entrance to the dorm and obliquely opposite to Cerone. He too was of mob affiliation. According to him, his driver taped him and turned him in. He got ten years and had five to go. He had been here for a year for medical reasons. I remember unknotting his returned laundry bag because he had serious vision problems. He said he had been waiting for an operation for some time since he had been at other medical prisons.

One day, they were talking about the mob between New York and Chicago, who was more enforcing. Frankie said, "In Chicago six for five or trunk music." I remembered reading about "trunk music" in "The Enforcer." For New York, Lou replied, "Anybody double-cross us is fucking dead." This was the only time mob actions were spoken out right. Tommy from PA was quiet, so quiet that he was actually feared by everyone. Word was that he looked out for the god father Cerone. Cerone opposed anyone smoking except Tommy, who was about fifty-four years old, and Cerone treated him like a son. He would go to the commissary with Cerone. When he returned, he did not leave the dormitory unless he went for meals, which he rarely did. He cooked most of his meals in our so-called kitchen, a room just outside the dorm with a refrigerator and a microwave. He was convicted on a twenty-year sentence and had seventeen to go.

Words around describe him as a capo and he acted to be feared. Tommy was really a nice guy if he wanted to be. He would give you anything you need as long as you return it. His and Cerone's lockers were full of everything. Cerone alone had two extra lockers. One time I returned a stamp I borrowed from Tommy. He did not like the idea of me bothering him about returning a postage stamp, which in my opinion was one of the most important items for the ordinary inmate, so he could mail a letter to a loved one. When I first arrived in the dorm, he asked, "Do you have shower shoes?" I said no, not knowing what he meant. He went to his locker, which was third from the foot of my bed, and gave me a pair of rubber slippers, which I returned with a new pair from the commissary in two weeks. I could not believe I was with such high profile guys. I was a little fish in a big pond. I would say to them, "I did white collar crime," so I could fit in.

I soon found out what "street" meant. It meant that you were not transferred here from a prison where you are already doing time, but that your conviction had just recently occurred and you left your home either voluntary or involuntarily and was placed into incarceration. The word "street" meant home, community, or outside the prison world that is free. "Down" meant how many years you had been in prison. In my case, I was down five for twelve months; the doctor was convicted for medicine prescription fraud, which falls into the category of illegal drugs and was sentenced to forty-two months.

He had arrived two months before me. He was a wealthy octogenarian who said he made his money charging the poor in Brooklyn only $10. He was so rich he would have his lawyer flown in to discuss his appeal. He had spent $500,000 in legal proceedings and another $500,000 towards his lawyer's specific performance due to outcome with his recent divorce from his young wife he had brought from Turkey, his original birthplace.

As mentioned before, he seemed lost like me in this different world. He was not liked by one or two guys in the dorm, but Ron would always defend him quietly by staring at the accuser of the doctor. Sometimes, the doc would say "look! mafia palace," responding to the fact that the mafia boys slept under the covers with no top on or shirt in the dead of winter, or about Cerone having his massage, which paid as much as $10 to someone younger and healthier from another area of the unit.

The mafia boys paid to get their haircut, laundry washed, and their bed made up. The doc had some respect for the mafia boys, but not for Frankie whom the \ doc nicknamed Paper-Clipper, meaning that Frankie, who had a large voice, was a small physical man about sixty-two who rubbed elbows with the more seasoned mafia guys because he was Italiano and was from Chicago. Frankie was a lower level guy in respect to Tommy or Lou. He knew the doc did not like him and he did not like the doc either. One day, the doc, wearing an ear aid, was talking a little loud, which bothered Frankie who shouted to the doctor to keep it down. Ron, a quiet man, turned around and said to Frankie, "We are having a conversation here and don't want to be disturbed." Wielding his cane as he lay back in the upright position in his bunk, he continued, "And if you don't shut your mouth, I will shut it for you," as usual with that strong southern accent.

I have never seen big mouth Frankie become so quiet, and as usual I smiled and looked at Ron. I cannot include everybody in my story, but some of the characters I felt were worth mentioning, like Big John, black and burly man from Chicago, about sixty-four, and was here for sixty days for fraud. I think the reason could be that the government could say they sent him to the prison because he was a large man. He did not use the dorm bathroom because Frankie had said that after he was finished due to stink, we might have to wait at least half an hour before going in to the bathroom.

Big John also showered at the west side. He was so upset that he would leave in the morning and never return to the dorm until count time at four. Then there was Big Jim, about forty, white and weighed about 500 pounds. He was here for his ninety-day sentence for credit card fraud. He came in with his breathing machine and a special wheelchair was adapted for him. Again the government had to prove its point but at a cost, because wherever he went his machine had to follow and a guard had to do the fetching and the dragging. Big John and Big Jim left before me. Big Jim always called me Misdemeanor by name. Ronnie was from Florida, but he lived in the Midwest, Missouri, and other places, and he worked in so many places and at so many jobs that one would think he would be about seventy years. But he was about fifty-two years. He was a swell guy to talk to, that is if he would speak to you. I enjoyed talking to him because I learned a lot about the prison system. He was convicted on drugs, his properties forfeited and was given fifteen years with eleven to go.

He and many others hoped for relief with the upcoming congressional action to address the double jeopardy issue in the spring of 1996, but lost due to the outcome of the decision. The issue was that if the government convicted and imprisoned a person, then turn around and took his property also, that person was put in jeopardy. But the ruling stated that if the property was acquired through illegal profits, the property is taken away because it was acquired illegally and the person is also punished by imprisonment for taking part of the crime. This was the way I interpreted the ruling.

Ronnie and many others hoped that the double jeopardy issue would either release them or restore his two million dollars that he lost with interest. He liked to read magazines about trucks and industrial auctions on any kind of equipment. Once he said to me, "Misdemeanor, you can get a plane for sixty." I told him, "Hell no," then he showed me the magazine. He had a great idea about hurricane damage; that is, putting up lumber yards in stress areas so big profits could be made for the need of lumber. The insurance companies would be paying for it. He spoke about estimating damage to homes, and being right on the scene as everyone is panicking and going the other way. You would be the first one in with your estimate and the damage control would be in process. I liked this part of the conversation because I am licensed in real estate and understand buildings and replacements cost.

There were two people I would very much like to be free, and Ronnie was one of them. I won't go into details of his conviction, but from reading his pre-sentence report, he got a raw deal about who was involved, when, and the type and quantity of drugs. When he was waiting for relief from the double jeopardy issue, I asked him, "Would you rather keep the million and do the rest of the time?" But by talking with him for some months now, I knew what his answer would be, "Hell no for as long as I am out I can always make money. I would rather be free, the money would come later."

The other person I would like to be set free was Pete, who would be discussed in my struggle that caused me to successfully leave Kentucky. We should still remember no matter how any of us felt about the injustices by the government that we are all guilty, otherwise we won't be here. About one month after arrival, Reggie and I met Al from Memphis for the very first time since in R&D. He was standing in the chow line. I called out to him about where he had been. He said he had been in the psychological unit and had been moved to a minimum attached unit, which allowed him to be in the population and to mix with other people as part of the healing process. Before, he was locked in twenty-four hours and his meals were brought to him. He also said the unit had its own clinic, because we wondered why we had never seen him at the clinic. He also said he spent several days at the city hospital outside with twenty-four-hour guards, and not only once but twice that he had to be taken there. He had a serious colonoscopy situation.

Two weeks later after we met, he was brought over to my unit and placed in a two-man room in the upper level on the west side. This transfer move was intended that he would be closer to the prison hospital upstairs. Many times in a week he had to be pumped out, sometimes through the nose in order to clean his colon. It would get so serious that he had to be rushed outside many times. I felt this was a terrible way to live in this world of ours, but he was guilty and that was all that matters. He did not speak to anyone in my unit at least not for a good while, and after it was found out what prison he transferred from, he was both feared and respected. I had told him where I was located, so he found me and visited me every day. He told me that he did not speak to anyone in the unit, not even his roommate who he thinks was afraid of him because of his quietness.

He finally discussed his life and times with me, but only a little at a time. He said that he ordinarily did not speak about his troubles because it made him upset, but I seem like someone he could relate to. I took my time and \ finally asked him how long he was at Maryland. At least this was what I thought he said when we first met at R&D in February, then he said, "Marion, Illinois." I asked him what happened, also stating to him that I did not like to pry into other people's problems. He replied, "You don't want to know," then he left. As he left, Ronnie heard the word "Marion" mentioned, so he said to me, "You know what is Marion?" I said no. "To go to Marion you must have killed someone or did something real bad," he continued. I did not know what to say when Al came to visit. He pushed my wheelchair all the way to chow and I avoided the issue. The men on the west side could not understand why he only spoke with me from the east side, and to make it worse, they could not understand why he would speak with a guy, with a Misdemeanor conviction when he was a guy facing life. That was when they found out about his criminal history.

One day he came by about ten in the morning and sat in my wheelchair while I lay in bed. He told me some of his past. He was convicted for arranging drug flow into America, though he was never found with any, but he was well known, lived a good life with a home in Florida and Tennessee, rented yacht vacations to the Caribbean and flew in charted jets. He even tried to run for congress in Florida. He was in his forties, light skinned and seemed like a person that did well in society. My conclusion was that this was one of the strikes against him. Also, he got large bank loans and dealt his business overseas. He felt he was framed by the white man who felt he may win in politics according to Al. To ensure a solid conviction, the government charged him with white slavery. He knew a lady of the night who happened to be white and gave her a ride to a stop on his way to Florida in his car. He was charged for taking a white woman across state lines for prostitution. I told him there was no such law. He told me to look it up, and I found it in the library as a title 18:2421 statute in criminal rules and procedure. Al was given life and was held in a Miami federal detention center. His whole world, his sweet life, his family all taken away in a New York minute and he could not take it. He just went plain crazy. He went berserk and tore up the place, cutting and injuring guards. Through the years he beat up guards and inmates and was beaten up in return. He was in constant rebellion, so he was taken to America's new Alcatraz, the super max federal prison in Illinois, where you rarely see sunlight. He was locked up in years of darkness, naked many of the times, and given bad food. Sometimes, he would be tied down on a bed with no fabric for weeks and he would be turned over to the next position for another week. He could not move, so his human waste remained with him. He became a look-a-like animal and his wife and children did not visit him anymore because they could not recognize him nor him them. Somehow his old friend, a lawyer, never gave up on him and after ten years, he was granted parole a few months before coming to Lexington.

Prison officials at Marion, Illinois knew he had only a few months to go, so they sent him to Lexington for medical treatment. In my opinion, it was a move a little too late because he needed a new stomach and colon. He could not eat solid food, only jello and ice cream and broth. One day, he ate something a little stronger and he was in the hospital that night. We went to church a lot, on Wednesdays, Sundays and Tuesdays to prayer service. He applied through the prison chapel to enter the ministry, which he would continue when he left prison. He had been speaking to his wife often since coming to Lexington. She kept the home and children together all those years. His son was now fifteen and the twin girls thirteen. He reminisced how he took them on sail boats that he managed himself from Miami to the Bahamas. We talked about how he would greet them. He did not know if he should visit his mother first. He left about one month after me. He had been trying to get me to go to the prison recreation yard. I finally let him push me to the yard. I just wanted to see what the yard was like before I left Lexington Kentucky.

Malignancy and Wrongful Imprisonment

The proceeding chapters dealt with my experiences, apprisals, and the infirmities I had seen within the prison system. My very own infirmities started with the accident in 1992, but the events that followed caused my health to deteriorate due to the intentional acts by the government to cause me harm and infliction of emotional distress. This endangered my health, but the government did not care. Their concern was to achieve a sure conviction even if they had to defy the law of exegesis by interpreting the charge to suit their purpose. Over and over again here in America, people are not prosecuted for what they may have done or not done, but they are prosecuted for who they are or what they have become.

On January 20, 1995, seven months since I had known I was being investigated, two government agents came to my house and gave me a summons to appear in court. They also told me I would be assigned a public defender and left. I thought that because the three of us all worked for the same organization, they were concerned about me, but little did I know I was being set up for a sure slaughter.

On February 2, 1995 I received a letter from pre-trial services. I had never heard about this kind of process, but I know what the word "pre" meant. The letter stated "a prehearing interview is necessary to assist us in furnishing the judge or magistrate with accurate and reliable information on your community and family ties to determine any condition of bail or release." The words "bail" and "release" gave me the shivers. I called the number that was given in the letter and was told that the pre-trial officer was on vacation. I called back when I was told to and the response was "just come in a little earlier on February 14."

Before I left home the morning of February 14, I got a call from the Postal Inspection office to get down town even earlier for processing. They fingerprinted and did my mug shots. I hopped back across the street to pre-trial and gave them all my financial information, including a mortgage-free house located by the New Jersey shore. On Valentine's Day, about 2:30 PM, and three hours since I left home, I was arraigned in federal court. Ten minutes after the arraignment, I was fingerprinted and mug shots taken again, but this time by the marshals. The court room was right around the corner from the Postal Inspection office on the same floor in the same building. At the initial appearance, the magistrate did not ask me if I could afford a lawyer, but said, "Mr. Joe Smoke will represent you for this proceeding." I was released on $10,000 recognizance bond and left.

One week later, I was called at home and a guy told me he was my assigned public defender and that the other lawyer was just filling in for him at the February 14 initial appearance. We met at the federal public defender's office for the first time a few days later and spoke about the charge. He opened a book, pointed to a page and closed the book instantly. He did the same at our next meeting, but never explaining what "levels" meant. I found out what it meant when I hired a lawyer several months later. My public defender said to me, "You took the money, didn't you?" I said, "Yes, but—," He interrupted, "If you go to trial you don't stand a chance, worse if the judge had a bad night, plea guilty and go on with your life, to work and everything." I said to him, "But that will give me a record," then he replied, "No, it will only be a misdemeanor and you won't have a record." But he lied. Later, during the guilty plea withdrawal process, I discovered that my public defender already had a guilty plea from the U.S. attorney sitting in his desk before I even first met him. What he was doing between the time we met and May 11, the next date, was working on me to the point where I would agree to plea guilty and he would have succeeded, which he did. When I signed the plea a few days before going to court, I noticed it had a stipulated date of March 16, or the deal was off. I pointed this out to him that the document would not hold and that it would be invalid because it was then the month of May. His response was, "Don't worry about that," but I was worrying about the whole damn nightmare I was going through.

In court, the magistrate asked me, "Do you want to give up your rights now and plea guilty?" I did not answer. I was sitting down because of my legs; I could not stand for any period of time. The magistrate asked me again and my public defender looked down at me as if he was silently instructing me to agree. I finally responded, "Yes, sir," knowing damn well I was not guilty and did not want to plea guilty.

My public defender lawyer then accompanied me to the probation department across the street. I thought that probation was my sentence, but I was not sentenced so why was I going to see the probation officer, the probation was a complete nightmare. I was told to bring in birth certificate, school diplomas and degrees, recommendations, and letters to the judge, all to be ready by May 30. When the public defender was crossed questioned by my new attorney why he accompanied me to the probation office, his response was that he ordinarily sends defendants to the probation office on their own, but he made an exception in my case because I seemed difficult to deal with and I was forty-one years old, and did not understand the American legal system. I would discuss in my next chapter what I believed his true motives were.

On May 5, 1995, I was diagnosed of having osteomyelitis in the legs, and was afraid of amputation. On May 26, more tests were done at the hospital. On July 5, 1995, I received a letter from the Department of Labor that all my benefits were terminated including medical because I had pled guilty. On July 28, the probation department presented the court a horrifying profile about me in its pre-sentence report (P.S.R), and recommended a one-year prison sentence. Sentence date was set for August 17. After I received my copy more than a week later I called the lawyer and confronted him about the plea and the probation department recommendation and the probation sentence that I was supposed to get. He said that I stated earlier about my property down the seashore, but I knew this was a lie, because it was in the transcript of February 4. The probation department also stated that I owned a property in Northern New Jersey., but I did not. I parted with that property six years earlier after my first divorce.

My legs were getting worn out in court that August afternoon. On the way out of court, in the corridor, he yelled, shouted and told me "Shut the fuck up," which was heard causing people and court officers to turn their heads and look in awe. He was walking away while shouting and I was hopping with my cane trying to catch up with him. At his office he told me to go to the Hall of Records and bring the deed showing I did not own the Northern New Jersey. property. I wanted to ask the public defender why he yelled at me, but I did not. Being a realtor, I know that all the probation office had to do was call the municipality where the property was located and give the address. They would have been told who the owner was.

My penalty was at Level 9. It went to Level 11, and letters from the prosecution of August 2 and August 10 recommended a stiffer sentence making it to Level 13, which is twelve months in jail. I felt my lawyer was not working for me, but for the government who also was paying him. He lied to me about not having a record because he knew that I did not understand the American criminal justice system, and he did not discuss the risks of pleading guilty.

The next day after the August 17 fiasco in court, I ended up in the hospital with a chronic attack in the legs. The next week the lawyer demanded I bring hospital records so to verify that I could not see him on the 18th with mortgage applications, bank papers and deeds. When he first picked up the telephone receiver, he said to me, "Where are the fucking papers?" Before our conversation ended, I asked him what the purpose of the papers was, because I did not see what the relevancy was. His response was, "The judge wanted it."

I visited the probation department on August 30 with the public defender present. I was on crutches, with food plastic bags wrapped around my feet because I could not wear shoes, slippers, nor socks. And cold air from air conditioners did not help either. How inhumane my lawyer and probation department were. I gave them everything they wanted. My lawyer then said to me, "You going to jail; you screw up." I could not believe him. Whose side was he on? In September, I hired a criminal attorney and my public defender became a potential government witness against me.

My new attorney challenged the probation officer's report and filed for an evidentiary hearing to withdraw the guilty plea. The magistrate said he did not see any grounds to have an evidentiary hearing, then my lawyer pointed out on page six of the plea colloquy on May 11 when the magistrate asked me twice before I answered yes to the plea. Under the revealed circumstances, the magistrate reluctantly agreed to allow the hearing, but I knew in my heart that December 27 day that I would lose at the evidentiary hearing scheduled for January 2, 1996, because the plan had to be carried out. After two days of testimony including that of my previous public defender for the government, the magistrate rejected my plea withdrawal. They were not going to have some hot shot well-dressed experienced lawyer come in and mess up and change a whole year of the government assault against me, so on January 3, 1996, he carried out what was expected; that was a twelve-month prison sentence, also rejecting downward departure for my extraordinary physical disabilities.

I almost went through the floor. I was never locked up in my whole life, no, not me, and I was taken away to the county jail where I stayed up all night. They made me put up my two houses for bail, both then having a mortgage and I was released the next day, January 4, 1996 for thirty days to surrender, but on January 29, the probation office called me and told me to be in Kentucky by noon of February 2. I told her it was not thirty days yet and why I was going to Kentucky, and she replied, "That's where you are being sent."

I was being taken away from my family and my community, so on February 2, 1996, I surrendered at the Marshall's Office in Newark at twelve noon. On my way down, I wrote a letter in desperation to the magistrate asking him to reconsider my health and not to take me away from my family and my children, but his clerk told me he would not respond to the letter. I wrote him twice before, or the 17th and the 24th of January 1996, asking him not to put ankle monitors on my feet because it would be embarrassing to me if my grandchildren asked me what they were when they came to visit me. I thought I would be allowed to serve my sentence at home, especially since I had my appeal in. I did not know they had other plans for me. No response were made in regards to those two letters, obviously!

A few days later, while at the county jail waiting to be transported, I was told to get ready for court. The marshals came and got me. My lawyer was in court. The magistrate requested a hearing (show cause order) why I should not pay the public defender's time, because since I hired a lawyer, I should pay the public defender's cost. My lawyer advised me not to oppose but to agree to pay it. He said it wasn't much, and that I could afford it, but I really couldn't. I was in debt. He also said that agreeing to pay should help his motion for me to be released pending appeal. The magistrate said he wanted to hear the show cause order motion first about the public defender's fees, then he would hear the second motion for release. My lawyer got up and said I would pay the public defender's fees. As soon as he said that, the magistrate said the other motion was denied. Yes, we were tricked.

Months later when I started to read "the federal rules of criminal procedure," I learned that the court must state its reason for accepting or rejecting a motion. My appeal was set for February 14, 1996, which seemed very fast. About the end of January, 30th to be exact, the prosecutor wrote the district judge in Trenton explaining he could not be ready so early and he did not know what grounds I had for an appeal. I wrote the judge from the county jail explaining to her that I did not have money to retain a lawyer. I owed my attorney a balance and could not pay him off, the reason why I filed the appeal January 11 *pro se*. On February 8, 1996, I was told at the county jail to gather my belongings because I was being taken downtown to be transferred, but for some reason I was returned back to the county jail. This gave me a chance to see my mother that

Saturday, since Saturday coincides with inmate visit according to last names. My mother cried. I was being taken away far and out of state. She said it was god's doing that I was delayed so that she could see me.

On February 13, 1996, after one year and eight court appearances, I was picked up at the county jail for departure to prison. One of the marshals who regularly took me back and forth since January 3rd imprisonment always put me in the van last with no manacles. He knew I could not walk well with my cane and back brace nor run away because I could not. He said to me, "Man, you fucked up, the magistrate [he called him by name] said he was not gonna send you to jail but you pissed him off. You should have kept your lawyer [meaning the public defender] and kept your mouth shut." I was sitting at the county jail officer's desk while he was shackling the other guys and talking to me. They all walked out leaving me sitting there. He came back and said smilingly, "We almost left without you. Let's go," and he helped me into the van as usual.

I told this to my lawyer three weeks later when I was in Kentucky and he wanted to know his name because it would greatly help my case. I told him it would be better if I did not disclose his name. I liked the guy. He was good to me and showed compassion and I did not want to mess up his career. He told me the truth. He was about thirty years old. I also knew it could cause serious legal problems and could make my situation even worse.

When we got to the Marshals Office, I was checked and padded down by another marshal in a visiting room where arrested persons could speak to their lawyers through a phone. We just used the room instead of the holding cell. I was put into a car with two other marshals. It seemed we were late for the plane, so they put on their sirens, called local enforcement in the area about traffic authority and they raced down the highway sometime driving on restricted areas. One would think I was a high profile convicted figure being taken in private to a private plane. A small private plane it was.

As I mentioned earlier, there were three others—two men and one woman—on the small plane. A marshal told my escorted marshal that I could not take my Bible and a regular-size envelope with me on the plane. He said the B.O.P. would not allow it. But that was a lie. Bibles and court papers are allowed at first arrival. All the transporting marshal had to do was to turn them over to the B.O.P. officials at arrival. In the envelope, I had sample of complaints to the appeal judge. I also documented events of lack of highly needed narcotic analgesic medications I was not getting until my lawyer called the county jail in New Jersey. I even documented daily activities at the jail of several personnel, including their names, information I could have used in my complaint for improper care due to my health circumstances. Before I entered the plane, the marshal told me it would be sent to my house. To this day, nothing came to the house except my medications that I had brought with me at surrender. I arrived at the Bureau of Prisons (B.O.P.) in Lexington Kentucky before noon and the next day would be Valentine's Day. Last Valentine I was in a federal court in Newark, New Jersey. This Valentine I would be spending in a federal prison in Southern United States. The evil doers had achieved their objective.

I Want to Be Free

I tried from a distance to raise money for the appeal. I wrote the judge again and asked her for more time to raise the money and she gave me thirty days. I finally got help, but not before I told my lawyer that he had a moral obligation to help me and that money was not everything. He said he needed the money. The money came through and on March 11, 1996; he informed that he was on record to represent me for the April 30th appeal argument.

When I was searching around for money during my bail pending surrender back in January, I found out who my friends really were. After thirty years of associating and now forty-two years old, I learned for the first time that people who don't have much money are the ones that want to help, and those that have more money want to hold on to their money and never want to part with it. Worse, if you are in jail, or suppose you lose the appeal, they would think it would be years before you could pay back or they would never see their money.

While the appeal process was in motion, Ronnie said to me one day what he thought I was really facing. He remarked, "I read your pre-sentence a few weeks ago and I don't think you are here for that little shit they are accusing you of." He paused. I did not know what he was getting at. He continued, "You want to hear what I think? I don't want to upset you." I replied, "No, go ahead," then he continued, "You were sent here because you tried to live like a white man." He stopped, moving his tongue in his mouth, looking down and up in reciprocity and at the same time tapping at his shoe with his cane. He continued, "You know what else, you went on and married a white woman and these are the reasons why you are here, not that little bit of money."

I was shocked, but I did not show it. His statement bothered me for two whole weeks. My attorney felt sure that the least we could get from the appeal was a two-level downward departure because the evidence of my property disclosure at the Rule 11 initial appearance was in the transcript, but the district judge said in the decision order that even if she gave me the two-level downward departure, I would still fall within the ten to fourteen months range, so she affirmed the magistrate's decision. I received it a few days before Memorial Day. My lawyer never received his copy. I called him June 1st and informed him about the decision. First he was shocked then mad about not being informed right away after the decision as customarily done from the judge's clerk, according to him.

During the Memorial Day weekend, I came upon an awful discovery, and after cross referencing and reading case studies, I knew I was about to leave Kentucky, but actually when I did not know. I studied the statute and case studies and then informed my attorney. My feeling of renewed hope became apparent and this was where Pete the inmate came in. He was what they called a kind of jail house lawyer, but he never went to law school. His experience came from spending fourteen months in a Brooklyn federal holding prison where he spent many days in the library. He rolled in the dormitory on May 2, 1996. He got Halbert's bunk. Halbert had moved to a two-man room. Not that he had seniority over the mafia boys for that privilege, but it was just that the mafia boys did not want to split up. Besides, they had more room to move around in the dorm, which was kind of private anyway, because they kept it that way. Besides, where would they hang their robes that they wore every day to any place in the unit? The black boys used to tease me when I roamed in my pyjamas that all I needed was my robe, also where and how the godfather could have so many lockers.

Pete only got out of his wheelchair to get into bed. He needed a bone operation he had been waiting a whole year for. In months since he arrived and to the time I left, he had not been consulted by an orthopedic surgeon who came in to the facility periodically. He was Jewish and a Canadian citizen, though he had married a U.S. citizen, had children and lived on for some twenty years after marriage, but never took U.S. citizenship. He did business all over the world including London and the Caribbean. He was an expert in setting up golf courses and dealings with real estate transactions. He had been down fourteen months on a seven-year sentence on drug money implication, though he never dealt in drugs.

At this point, I want to mention that middle-aged men convicted on the drugs statute were not drug users; they were convicted by association just like one guy, twenty-nine years, in a wheelchair and from Kentucky, who was serving twenty years for having a marijuana farm. Pete always seemed knowledgeable about court proceedings, federal statutes and guidelines. All the time while helping others the best he could, he was working on the Strasbourg treaty transfer, which is an agreement between the United States and some foreign countries to allow convicted people to serve out their sentences in the countries of their origin rather than the country where they committed the crime. It is of some beliefs that these persons convicted feel they would be treated fairly and with dignity and compassion if they were in their own homeland. Some of the countries hosting the sentences can even reduce the sentence once the inmate arrives. According to Pete, in Canada, the sentence would be one third of what it was in the U.S. If he were to succeed within a few months since arriving Kentucky, he would have served out his sentence which included the fourteen months he had already served. He also said that the Canadian criminal justice system is more caring than the U.S., because it does not believe in keeping families separated for long periods of time because it destroys them and turn immediate and extended families into dysfunctional families.

Pete will read pre-sentence reports of inmates and would tell them whether they were "finished," or that their lawyer or the prosecutor screwed them real good. He said to me, "You are here on a misdemeanor charge! That is illegal. It is against the law to place a misdemeanor with felons. You should have been given probation and a $5,000 fine, or thirty days in a county jail and a $500 fine. Called your lawyer and tell him he fucked up. You got no business here."

After reading my presentence report, he said to me, "The judge, public defender, the post office people, prosecutor were in this together." He further went on, "Your appeal would be denied." I said, "Why?" He replied, "Look, they play golf together, party together, call each other on the phone. I can just see it. The appeal judge calling up the judge he is supposed to go against, 'Hey, you know so and so, that black bastard thinks I am going to get him off. Yes, you did screw up about the house down the shore, he was telling the truth, but don't worry I will take care of it,'" Pete continued. "That is what's gonna happen. I could be wrong, but I don't think so. Look, they went into things like your property, divorce, your real estate license and turn them into legal issues in order to strengthen their case against you and to assure a conviction. All those investigators, they nailed you good."

Two weeks later he was right. That's when I received the decision in the mail from the district court. To be exact, I received it at 9:40 PM, Tuesday, May 28th. I had missed the 7:30 PM mail call. I was shocked and had a sleepless night. I waited till the next day to tell Pete. He saw how much I was disappointed because I wanted so much to be free. An hour later just before lunch, he wheeled over to me and asked one question: "You said it was a magistrate." I told him yes. Then he asked, "Did he read you your rights before the trial?" I responded, "What rights, what trial?" "You mean to tell me you were not read your rights in court." Again, I asked him "What rights?" "Your rights to be tried by a judge," Pete replied. I told him I did not understand. He said he would look into his locker and check something. Pete had a lot of legal books and periodicals.

The next day he showed me a soft cover book called *American Jurisprudence* with about a thousand *habeas corpus* case studies and there it was, "the power of magistrates" under 636(c) title 28, so I wheeled down to the library and got help locating the title 28 series under the United States Code Annotated (USCA). I found the book and was shocked from reading the disclosures. I read the case studies even the additions in the pocket parts to make sure there was consistency in conformity. I read over and over about U.S. attorneys, attorney general, probation or parole officers, U.S. marshals, all about their duties and appointments. I read the entire section about magistrates and judges and other court officers, and then I finally knew that I was indeed set up for the slaughter. I was intentionally, willfully, and wrongfully imprisoned by the government because their evil doings had to be carried out.

Revelations and Demagoguism

The entire proceedings from February 14, 1995 to imprisonment were all illegal because the magistrate was without authority. On Monday, June 3, 1996, I called my attorney. He said he could not believe and it could not be true. He could not believe that the Article III decision-making policies of a magistrate had not been carried out when I first appeared before him. So my attorney drove the seventy miles to the state capital where my records were and read the court files. He wrote me an overnight air letter telling me I was correct. The magistrate violated title 18.3401 and Rule 58 of the federal rules of criminal procedure. The prosecutor and my federal public defender all knew the rules, but never saw it carried out. My conclusion was that the government was such in a rush for their own justice that they did not stay on the procedural course and making sure they left no stones unturned. Now everyone would be exposed, but they made sure I suffer some pain first before I ever see New Jersey again.

Upon disclosure of what I found, I decided to recapitulate the events by dates, by occurrence, who said what, how, what, and all the court appearances, eight of them in all and notwithstanding all the above, but also what was said in the library and the dormitory—I could only conclude a revealing picture of demagogy. When I put the pieces together, they did fit. I know my discovery would shake up the legal authority and the criminal justice system and that would derail the objectives of the evil doers. There would be lot of talk behind closed doors and judges exposed whether they intentionally did what was done or lacked or was just ignorant of the law. The news shocked other inmates in the dorm and the few I spoke with when I visited the library, which became visitation on a daily basis. Jokingly, the guys, especially Al from Tennessee, called me and Pete "Cochrin and Bailey," then about a month before I left, another guy was added to the jail house team, and the name Shapiro was added. The three of us could be seen wheeling down towards the dormitory and along the hallway corridors to the library.

Paper trail showed a cruel and disturbing picture of the government's assault against me. To put it in a clear picture, I will scantly go back and trace some of the events that would show conformity and demagoguism. When I went to college, I learned something in my engineering class something called "the truth table," applied to digital logic applications. The truth table means that something or an act may, can, likely, probably and definitely could be true. Remember on January 20, 1995 when two inspectors came to my house and gave me the summons to appear February 14? Well, at that time, I was told that a lawyer would be assigned to me. How did they know I could not afford a lawyer? Then there was the letter from pre-trial services dated February 2, 1995, which concluded "if you are financially unable to obtain counsel, the court will enquire into your financial status under oath. If it determines you cannot afford an attorney, the court will approve the appointment of counsel on your behalf."

I did give my financial information on the day I was told to go in, and that was the same day of my court appearance because they were not available before that date. I mentioned in the report that I owned a mortgage-free vacation home at the New Jersey shore. The magistrate had the report in his possession before I appeared in front of him. He went ahead and presented a lawyer who happened to be in court. He never asked me if I could afford a lawyer. You remember I was contacted by the public defender's office informing me that he was my appointed attorney and not the other guy that stood in for him. Well, when I was hauled into court about the public defender fees, the public defender made out a staff time report showing dates and length of time he spent on my case. The report indicated he was working on my case about two weeks before I ever first went before the judge. How could this be possible? The report also stated, "please note that services were performed in connection with this matter prior to February 14, 1995 in anticipation of this office's appointment as counsel." How could this be possible? How could the federal public defender's office anticipate I would need their services without even knowing my financial situation? The answer had to be that it was planned that my legal defense would be done inside, which was within the federal system and no outsiders.

The public defender is a federal employee. You remember him telling me that I won't have a record if I plead guilty to the misdemeanor. Well, he lied. What he did not tell me was that it was a class A misdemeanor, which is one step below a felony. Then there was the written plea agreement, which he had in his desk drawer before I even first went down to see him. The agreement had my name and an expiration date or the offer would be withdrawn. This was clearly stated in the plea offer. I signed it a month and a half beyond the expiration date. Looking back, I realize the expiration date was just a gimmick, for the only thing that mattered was my signature at any date before appearance in court on May 11.

Then there was the evidentiary hearing of January 2nd and 3rd, 1996, when the public defender testified against me. He said he ordinarily did not accompany a defendant to the probation office, but he made an exception in my case. As I remember that day at the probation office, he answered most of the probation officer's questions for me. He would turn to me at times and say "right" in anticipation of my nod in affirmation towards his answers. All the time, I was confused especially when he told me on the way while walking to the probation office that in no way, shape or form that I should, when we got there, indicate I really did not want to plea guilty, because the probation officer would recognize the doubt and the outcome of my case could be worse because the deal would be called off. You recall how he cursed me over the phone and in the hallway at the courthouse on August 17. He and everybody else were frustrated that things were not going as expected like I would be done with on that day. But I knew why they were going after my property, but he would not tell me except "the judge wanted it." What they were trying to achieve was to fine me $100,000; fine and a year in prison and to hell with a probationary sentence. They had a guilty plea and they were going all the way for the slaughter.

Paper trail and investigative memorandum from the government showed a convincing picture that the government gauged my legal representation in anticipation that the federal public defender would eventually convince me to plea guilty and they got what they wanted, because after non-compliance by the U.S. Department of Labor to previous memoranda, the government presented a post-plea memorandum and the Department of Labor finally had to comply to terminate all my health and financial benefits by letter to me on July 3, 1995 on account of the guilty plea. My public defender was a very ineffective counsel. He had to know all my benefits would be terminated should I plea guilty, that is why he told me that I should find a job when I told him the government stopped paying me by letter of July 3rd. The entire month of June and from Kentucky, I kept calling my claims examiner at the Department of Labor in New York about not receiving any checks, but they made all sets of excuses, like the checks are being processed or the forms had not arrived from the middle man in New Jersey. They lied. My public defender deprived me the opportunity to balance the risks and benefits of not pleading guilty and going to a trial.

When a pre-sentence report is prepared, the law states that the defendant must see it within ten days. My public defender did not discuss the P.S.R with me within those ten days from the date of preparation, which was July 28, 1995. I also remember him making remarks such as "Why don't you sell that property you have by the shore? Don't give me that shit about you are not about material things." He said this because I remarked that the government seemed more interested in material things instead about the charge. His remark was made after the plea was entered.

The court violated my rights by accepting a plea before a pre-sentence investigation had been completed. Under the federal sentencing guidelines, Section 6 Bi., it clearly states that the court (meaning the judge) must defer acceptance of a plea agreement until the court has had an opportunity to consider the pre-sentence report. Except, unless the defendant waives his rights to this rule and lets the court accept his plea and the report follow later. As you have been aware through my story, I had no rights.

At the oral arguments on December 27, 1995, to determine whether an evidentiary hearing would be allowed to withdraw my guilty plea, the magistrate finally acknowledged to my new retained lawyer how he (the magistrate) had to ask me twice about pleading guilty according to the Rule 11 plea hearing as indicated in the plea colloquy. This was enough evidence and very transparent about my involuntariness to plea guilty. According to American jurisprudence law, to prove involuntariness, the defendant must show fear of possible consequences of not pleading guilty, destroyed the ability to balance the risks and benefits of going to a trial in front a jury of his peers. I did show fear. The magistrate ignored that it was quite obvious I did not want to plea guilty when he had to ask me twice and I hesitated to answer. He only agreed to allow the hearing not because he thought I had a chance, but because it was quite obvious he had to ask me twice and that was recorded in the colloquy. I did not even think about New Year's Eve, only about the evidentiary hearing on January 2, 1996. After two days of hearings, he denied my withdrawal of the plea and sentenced me. He said he did not believe me. But he believed the public defender, the government's star witness. The public defender said in court that I had told him I wanted to plea guilty. I did not. He lied. I also remember the magistrate's last words at the August 17 appearance, "I don't buy it, this is the end, the buck stops here," and a lot more derogatory terms about me, such as how I lived a life of deception. This hurt me real bad, because I am the opposite of this remark. On January 3, 1996, one of his statements were: "His transparent attempt to manipulate our criminal justice system." I found this blatant remark not only untrue, but bias and exclusionary. I felt he was saying this because I am a foreign national though I have been a United States citizen for twenty years. And finally in February at the show cause order hearing, he rejected my attorney's motion under Rule 38 of the Federal Rules of Criminal Procedure (FRCP), which means to stay out on bail pending appeal. My conviction was not for a violent offense and I was definitely not a threat to the community nor a flight risk. The rule of law clearly states that a court must state its reasons for accepting or rejecting motions. It must state its reasons for a decision. The magistrate broke that rule and that law.

When I had filed for an appeal within ten days of conviction on January 3, 1996, my attorney thought the fee was about $110, but the clerk told me there was no fee. What I discovered reading title 28 USCA and 636(c) was that the appeal had to be handled by a district judge instead of the Court of Appeals in the third circuit. The reason was that the conviction arose out of proceedings conducted by a magistrate instead of a district judge. Title 18:36(c), title 18:3401 and Rule 58 of the Federal Rules of Criminal Procedure were all violated by the magistrate. All my court appearances, imprisonment, including the decision of the appeal, were all illegal. Never did the evil doers thought the tables would turn? They were in a rush for their justice and to humiliate, malign and demagogue an American of color. In America, race and criminal justice are explicitly interrelated.

The Price of Departure

On June 7, 1996, my attorney filed a motion on Rule 4 of the Local Appellate Rules (LAR) due to excusable neglect to file for an appeal within ten days to the district judge, who affirmed the May 21 order. His request was granted because he did not receive a copy of that order in time. He did not even know about the decision until I called him from Kentucky and told him that I received my copy on the 29th. He apprised the court about the magistrate's lack of authority as a substantial issue to be raised at the appeal to the third circuit. This was the first time the district judge realized she affirmed a proceeding that was illegitimate. I ponder if all the judges read all the documents in all cases, because if this is true, then in my case the issues would have been devoid.

My attorney was happy that we now had a case against the government because he felt I was dealt unfairly by the magistrate, who he also felt as being very biased, and the affirmation of his decision was absolutely incorrect and a stab in the heart. He offered to handle the appeal *pro bono*. I concluded that the outcome of the district judge's affirmation was due to the lies and misrepresentations by the U.S. attorney and the probation department.

My case was an unusual one. Here I spent five and a half months in prison, which was illegal, and my health had been greatly endangered due to the government's conquest to convict me. How could this all be changed and turned around? I knew it would not be easy. On June 13, 1996, the arbitration branch of my union that was fighting for my job back decided to concur with the government that I should lose my job. The union made this decision because they did not hear from me by their letter to me dated May 27, 1996, requesting to hear my complete side of the charges against me. This letter was sent to my house in N.J. instead of in Kentucky. When I returned to N.J., the union told me they never knew I was outside the district of N.J. and the government never told them.

As early as June 7, the government knew there was a ninety-nine percent chance that I would be leaving Kentucky due to the legal issues that came to light. They also knew this to be true on June 13, the day the union would make its decision as indicated in the May 27 letter, a copy which the government also had. Although they had an obligation to disclose factors pertaining to me as the disputed party, the government intentionally withheld information from the union that they had me imprisoned outside of N.J.

You see, the government had two agendas; one was that I be convicted and imprisoned, the other was that I lose the fight to win my job back. They succeeded in both. After reading my attorney's letter to the court, Pete said to me, "Tell your lawyer to stop stalling. All he has to do is to go in to the head man, you know, the guy in charge of the magistrate, tomorrow at 9 o'clock and say, 'Hey, Charlie, your people put my man in jail illegally and I want him out now, today, this afternoon.'" Pete would not even break a smile when he was talking. He was serious.

On July 3, 1996, the government consented by letter to the third circuit to withdraw the conviction against me. The government confessed the ERROR statute. They knew the Court of Appeals would overturn the conviction. In their letter they stated how I tried to abate my sentence and many ill will remarks about me. They were just plain mad. They concluded: "However the defendant is correct, I have asked the prosecuting attorney to have the defendant brought back to N.J. and he can be tried on a felony if he wishes." How can anybody wish to be tried on a higher charge arising out of the same circumstances? That is double jeopardy and they knew it. They did not think we were dumb enough to accept. The letter's last sentences stated: "He would require a substantial bond." I said to myself that they were out of their minds. Bond for what?

On July10, there was oral argument in Trenton because the third circuit remanded the case back to the district court. I told Pete and his response was, "You have been here a whole month now since your lawyer found out. Tell him to cut this crap and get you out of here. Call him now. Call him every day." I was wondering why there was a hearing when the government admitted wrongdoing. I thought that was the way things are done to be formally on record, but never did I know it would put me on a three-week painful and humiliating experience.

On the morning of July 11, 1996, at seven in the morning, the hack came and told me to pack my things. I did not go down for breakfast that morning. I had coffee and crackers in the dorm since six because I knew I was leaving that day. I was just waiting for the final word. I had to be in R&D by nine. Pete was at the west side TV viewing room. There was no air conditioning on the east side, our side, so we would spend as much time on the west side. I wheeled over and nodded to Pete and he knew. We both wheeled over back to the east side, to the dorm and I gave him almost all of what I had, including, unused shorts, socks, documents, clippings, prison complaint forms, all my coffee and condiments.

One of the inmate companions took me and my duffle bag to R&D, then he left wishing me goodbye. He was a nice guy from North Carolina. Many times it was difficult for me to comprehend his speaking, not because he was part American Indian. He gave Cerone a lot of back massages. At R&D the hack put me in street clothes, a pair of new blue jeans and blue long-sleeve cotton shirt, then he locked me in a cell. At first I couldn't understand it, then it came to me that the government was not going to let me go, oh no, not that easy.

When I built up enough will, I asked the guard what the problem was. I was told I was being picked up by U.S. marshals on a detainer. I said, "What detainer?" "A warrant," he replied. You see, the day before on July 10, the prosecutor convinced the district judge that the rule of law would be violated if I was not brought back in front of the same magistrate in N.J.; otherwise, I would have impunity, so I was arrested in prison by the marshals. I was shocked. The R&D supervisor told the marshals that I could not have leg irons because I could not walk, so I was helped out of my wheelchair and my left hand was shackled to my waist allowing my right hand free to ambulate with my cane. The R&D supervisor asked the marshals, "You people going to see him get home?" They replied, "No, we are just taking him in front of the magistrate, ten minutes the most, he is out and on his own." Then I interrupted, "How will I get home?" They responded, "You can catch the bus at the terminal," then I asked, "How will I get to the terminal?" The marshals replied, "You can take a ride. The R&D supervisor then asked me, "You have any money?" I said yes, $46.00 in the commissary, but I don't have it. I thought when someone leaves here, his money is given to him." "Yes," he replied, "but there was not enough time for the business to prepare it. You are an immediate release and the office just opened."

At release from prison, an inmate is given bus or plane ride back to his home at the prison's expense, but since I was put into marshal custody, I was now outside the prison's jurisdiction and the prison's responsibility to see me home is therefore waived. The government was just interested in its objective and to hell with me. When we got to downtown Lexington, which took seven minutes by car, I was placed in a holding cell. I don't know if they felt sorry for me for I seemed lost, so they allow a free phone call to my lawyer in N.J., but he was not in and his secretary could not honor my request to have him send me a plane ticket. I was sure I was leaving in ten minutes like the marshal said before, but I was dead wrong.

About half an hour later, I was told "Let's go," and was led out of the building to another car where I met two different marshals and we left. Before we took off, I asked the first two marshals what the problem was and the reply was, "No judges are here today, they are all off. You have to go to London, not far." Was this a holiday or something? Where the hell is London?

And why am I going to England. This is the only London I know?

The court house did seem small and quiet. Maybe it was a holiday in Lexington. Everything in Kentucky looked small to me except the big house, which I believe is big in every state. So we drove. I read the miles and signs and saw a lot more farms. I counted seventy miles and one and a half hours. As we pulled into London, I was asked by one marshal, "Where did you work and what did you do?" I don't know if he was testing me or what, but I told him. He kept chewing his tobacco then he continued, "I don't know what is with you people in N.J. You have a prosecutor mad as hell and hate to lose," he paused, "to turn around and charge you for the same thing!" I kept quiet, then the driver said to me, "You hungry? I am stopping at McDonalds? Want anything?" I responded with a Mac, fries and a Sprite.

We got to the court house which looked more like a rich southern home. I was put in a holding cell on the first floor right next to the marshal's office, and the court room was right around the corner. I asked the marshal to call the airline and find out how much the ticket was, and it was $350. I thought that was kind of high for one way, but it was peak time. I was assigned a public defender and I did not know why I would need a lawyer. We spoke for five minutes and the public defender said that he did not understand why I was being charged on a charge that had been dismissed. He told me I would go in front of the judge in five minutes, which would have been 1:30 PM. It came and went. Then he came back and told me I had to see a probation officer first and I asked why. His response was that the judge needed it for pre-trial purposes. Something told me that I was about to go through another nightmare as I had in New Jersey and everything seemed wrong. All I wanted was to get home. I was in pain from that long ride and my back pain had increased.

The probation officer came in the cell, which was very clean. It was like being in a house with tiled floor except the room was a cage. The probation officer, not more than twenty-five years old, asked about family ties and financial information, which I believed was not much except my family because my properties were being foreclosed. I asked him what was all this information for, and he replied, "The judge wanted it," then I said for what and he said "For your bail."

At 2:30 PM, the public defender came back and told me "the judge won't see you today because he needs some more information on you from New Jersey," then I asked him where I would be spending the night and he said, "Probably here or the county jail," and he left saying, "I would see you tomorrow." Before I was taken to the county jail, I was fingerprinted and photographed by the marshals, and the one chewing the tobacco said, "I guess they want some information from the prosecutor in N.J."

Now I know I would have a serious problem. I was taken to the county jail with another white guy about twenty-five, who was in the cell with me. He was busted for drugs and bomb-making materials. His girl friend locked up in the other cell was to be let go if he told the judge he was guilty, so she could go on and raise their three-year-old child the next ten years without him. He cried how he messed up her life and took full blame for it because if he didn't plead guilty, both of them were going down. At least this was what he said his lawyer told him, at the county jail, a filthy place.

I sat on the concrete floor for three hours before I was taken upstairs. I was told by the jailer that they did not have the accommodation for a guy like me with the type of health problems. He said the only place available was the maximum security unit where all the killers and thieves were. I was put in a big cell area that had individual cells for two. The area was like their own recreation, ten-by-fifteen space with a TV and a table with two benches. All ten of them could not sit at the same time because there would not be enough room. The jailer came back upstairs and put me in a cell by myself because the other prisoner was using the bottom and I could not climb to the top bunk, and he surely had seniority over me. Thanks to one of the "baddest" prisoners in that unit, because he called the jailer by banging on the intercom unit, which created a feedback to the control tower. He told the jailer I could not climb because of my medical condition, and the jailer complied. Mike was that guy and he was from Chicago. He said that he had been there five years waiting on his trial for murdering a woman in Kentucky. He felt that politics and the prosecutor's re-election had an impact on his case to begin. He gave me soap, toothbrush and tooth paste and we played chess, which seemed that he liked very much. I have not played chess in years, so I lost all the games. I think it was good I lost because he loved every bit of it. Supposed I knew how to play well . . . he may not have liked that and this could have made it bad for me, so it worked out well all around.

I called Patricia about 8:30 PM in N. J. and she agreed to send me a ticket to be picked up at Lexington airport for the next day, departing at 4:30 PM. She was happy I was out *per se* and was on my way home. She had to take her autistic son and herself to the doctor the next day, but she would get it done. I did not sleep that night. The next day at nine I was taken back to the court, but this time there was another marshal along with the tobacco-chewing marshal. The assigned public defender again remarked, "I don't understand why you are being charged on a charge that had been dismissed." He then said that the pre-trial report was not good. The probation officer that prepared the report indicated that I was a flight risk and the judge would deny bail and that I should waive detention hearing because it could be two to three weeks before it would be heard, which could mean a longer suffering.

I was shocked about hearing the flight risk thing. How could I be a flight risk now when my conviction was withdrawn and not when I was on a thirty-day bail pending surrender back in January to enter the penal system? Then the public defender said, "No, the prosecutor in N.J. had something to do with it." I knew it. I knew this was a set up and there was vindictiveness to malign and demagogue, and to make me suffer before I ever see N.J. again.

After the Rule 40 hearing, the magistrate then put me in the custody of the marshals, who took me back to the county jail, but this time I was kept downstairs where I spent two hours on the concrete floor sitting. I knew all this coldness was adding more damage to my already very sick musculoskeleton system. The marshals took me and my belongings, which they transferred from one car trunk to another the day before, but had kept them overnight in the same car that brought me to the county jail.

What I am trying to say was after I left the magistrate, they knew that the chewing marshal at least would be taking me out of London. I was not alone. Remember the long hair hippy looking twenty-five-year-old? Well, he and a black man about the same age from New York, both bound hand and feet, rode with us back past Lexington into Frankfurt, Kentucky, where I spent eleven horrifying days, twenty-four hours within concrete enclosure and with not much clothing but a short-sleeved shirt and pants from the jail.

I called Patricia and explained my dilemma. I told her I did not know when I would return exactly and that I would be brought back by the government and that she should get her money back. She thought at first I was calling her from N.J. She explained the fatigue of taking two busses that day, missed her appointment with the doctor, so she could get to a travel agency for the transaction. It was all in vain. It was too late to get in touch with my attorney back home. I would have to wait until Monday. I looked back at the events of the past two days and the fact that I was still in Kentucky made me very angry. The more I thought of it the more it seemed true that the government was hell bent to carry out its evil ways.

The prosecutor in Kentucky seemed too knowledgeable about my case. It was obvious the N.J. prosecutor briefed him well. He was a tall square-looking man with glasses and reflected the likewise personality on his N.J. counterpart, nerd-like looking. At the Rule 40 hearing, he got up and said, "I was on the phone with the U.S. attorney and the magistrate in N.J. and they requested $60,000 bail." How could they request a specific amount? As I said before, a court must state its reason. They knew back in N.J. that I had that much in equity and wanted to make sure they tied up everything I had. Under the Federal Rules of Criminal Procedure, when someone is arrested in a jurisdiction for an offense in another jurisdiction, he must be taken to the nearest magistrate forthwith in the arrested jurisdiction. Ordinarily, everyone would say, "you are going in front of the judge," but there is a big difference between a magistrate and a judge. I just want to point this out, as a matter of fact, it was the main reason why I was released from Lexington.

I called all my relatives and informed them where I was and what happened. I started to get numb in the legs. They were becoming weaker and weaker. There were no hot foods, no pills after the first three days and twenty-four hours lockdown. One of the guards who seemed concerned said to me, "I don't know why marshals bring sick people here. This is not for sick people." Both knees and ankles began to swell and I begged for a wheelchair. The nurse said they had none, neither crutches. She lied. I saw crutches at the rear in the pill-room where the pills were given. She told me I had to see the doctor who came in once a week every Monday, and I told her, "Today is Monday." She replied that I could not see him because I had to have a request slip in prior to Monday. "I just came in Friday afternoon," I told her. She finally said to me, "I am not your mother," which was enough for me to say no more.

I dragged myself back to my cell and called my lawyer at 8:30 AM. He was upset I was still in Kentucky. He thought I was home. I explained what happened since I spoke with him July 10, and it was now July 15, and I had been in two county jails and this was my fourth day at Frankfurt. He said he would call the public defender in London, KY and find out what happened. I asked him, "Why you didn't tell me a warrant was signed at hearing on July 10?" His response was that he fought like hell to get me released and that the misdemeanor charge still was in effect. Though I thanked him as always, I was a little upset that the prosecutor was still doing it his way and was getting away with it. Then I said to him, "You want to admit now that this whole thing has become personal between him and me?" He replied that he could not comment for he is a professional. I know he did not want to make me feel any worse, but he did voice his opinion vehemently when we met two weeks later.

I would not mention his remarks about the government the magistrate, and the prosecutor in N. J., but I can assure you they were not in any good taste. He called the marshals' headquarters in Kentucky and explained my condition that my health was at risk because I had two heart attacks and that I could die, or words to that effect. I was constantly in contact with the lawyer in London, KY, which was a toll call because it has a different area code. His office accepted all my calls. He told me that the magistrate in London KY had ordered my return to N.J. "forthwith," and which meant very soon like a day or two and that they were violating that order. He told me the marshals said they would have me there soon, but this did not happen for another week, and I know the government back home was enjoying every bit of my suffering.

I shared the American tragedies while in Kentucky from February 13 through July 2, 1996. From the church burnings, to the value jet crash down into the Florida everglades, then there was the inconceivable plane crash death of commerce secretary Ron Brown in Bosnia, followed by flight 800 in New York, which took over 200 lives, and finally the Atlanta bombing. As an American citizen, I shared the pains of the families as I was going through my very own. During the time at the Franklin jail in Frankfurt, Kentucky, I suffered a chronic attack on my right foot, which was very bad for me because this foot carries most of the body. The left side was the damaged side from the accident. In 1998, I had been aware through the doctors the past few years that the right side would get weaker due to additional burden to ambulate. I continued to drag my feet. I asked to be taken to the hospital, but the jail guards said they could not do that and they were not going to call the marshals either, because the marshals must have thought it was okay to bring me there. The previous guard was off for about three days. I only felt comfortable to speak to him. He seemed a little caring. He happened to be on that day, Monday, July 22, when I left his jail and Kentucky. One of the marshals (male) refused to take my belongings to the van, so that same previous jail guard, who happened to be on duty that day, responded that he would mail my belongings to my home, but this would take two months before I received it. The other marshal just happened to be the woman who picked me up at Blue Grass airport on February 13 when I first arrived in Kentucky.

I finally left Kentucky at 2:30 PM on a marshal plane. There was a segment on Sixty Minutes television broadcast in 1996, I believe, but definitely a follow up in August 1997 about why the U.S. marshal service take off every day from Oklahoma to move prisoners all over the country. The response as to why prisoners are moved around seemed very bizarre not only to the interviewer but to me taking into account what I had seen, but I won't comment any further as to the reasons. There were about 100 prisoners shackled hand and feet with little or no room to move. How cruel this seemed to me. I asked to sit at an aisle seat so I can get to the bathroom due to my urinary incontinence problems. The marshals always know the criminal status of an inmate and I was at the lowest of any one. Besides, I could not walk and I had to get to my nitroglycerine in case of an emergency. This medication was with me since I left Lexington. I thought everybody was going to New Jersey and New York, but the plane touched down at Harrisburg, Pennsylvania. I thought then there were PA prisoners. I only knew it was Harrisburg because I saw the name at the airport. Marshalls never discuss destinations at departures. I was told the reason for this was because of interceptions in the past.

At 4:30 PM, the plane took off and would not stop. With experience traveling in the past at 400 to 600 miles an hour, I estimate how many miles we had traveled so far departing Harrisburg. It seemed we should be in N.J. at least two hours ago, but the plane still would not stop. At about eight in the evening, it did stop, but before it did it seemed that there was a problem landing. Sitting at the back gave a good view of the wings. The guy closest to the window, spoke out quietly that a piece of the wing had broken off, which could be seen and it looked like it just happened. At that moment, I felt I would never see N.J. A few marshals sitting two seats behind me, which was actually the last seats, looked to me like they too were worried because they became very quiet. Maybe they were not worried that the plane was operating with a broken wing known to them, but to this day I doubt it because I would be on that plane again and I did not see the broken wing because I looked for it and it was not there. It was either fixed or it was another plane.

I could not believe what I was hearing from the prisoners in front, side and behind me, but they were correct we just landed in Oklahoma, all the way into America's heartland and many moons, as it seemed to me farther away from home. The marshals radioed in to have a wheelchair brought to the plane exit, which seemed like a regular gate at a regular airport. I could not drag my feet anymore and the marshals saw that, or they would have had to carry me. I was put with about twenty people in a holding cell for two hours before I was processed, which included mug shots and all. I had to take all my clothes off and told to spread eagle. I said to the hack, "Don't you see I am in a wheelchair?" "Everybody has to do it," he replied. We had to give up all our clothes including shorts which were all new. I had on two. We were given old used underwear. I could have got germs. In my eyeglass case, I had a few stamps and he told me he had to throw them in the garbage. I told him I bought them from the commissary a few weeks ago in at the BOP in Lexington. He said he did not care and that they were considered contraband, which is illegal. I then said to him, "I am not an inmate of the Bureau of Prisons, so I am not subjected to any rules of the BOP. I was released and the marshals are taking me back home to N.J." Then he replied, "You can get a shot if you refuse to get rid of the stamps and you can get more time." I told him he could have the damn stamps. I wanted to challenge him, but all I was concerned about was getting home.

Looking back, I wished I did. A shot is when an inmate violates a serious prison rule including verbal assault to a guard. Seasoned inmates never worry about shots, which if accumulated, got an inmate a few days or weeks in segregation. Some prisoners welcome shots, which give them the easy way out of prison work. I saw one inmate at Lexington refusing and cursing the kitchen guard, so he did not have to work in the kitchen, which is considered the most degrading job. He got two weeks in the hole. Hole is a term used for segregation.

Finally, I was put in a cell on the second floor for handicap. The irony of being in Oklahoma was this facility is the BOP, and though I was released July 11 of my sentence and conviction, I was still being treated as if I was a convict doing time because I was being referred to and processed under my prison inmate number given to me February 13, almost six months earlier. How could I still be a convicted prisoner when I had my conviction terminated?

The next day, I called both my lawyers, in N.J. and London, Kentucky, and they both were shocked at me being there. "What are you doing in Oklahoma?" My N.J. lawyer asked. It had been then a few days that I had no medication. What about my TB situation? Medication obsolescence, according to the BOP doctors at Lexington, could be dangerous to a person's health. Maybe they mean those dam I.N.H. pills for TB. My nitro was left in my clothes, which they kept, because they knew I had to be in N.J. by the 29th for my appearance and they could not mail my clothes back home as they did back on February 13, because now I was not staying with the BOP as I did back then.

The next morning, I saw the nurse and told her I had no medications for days especially for high blood pressure and for TB. A few hours later, another nurse came looking for me about my TB, but not the medications. She came to take a TB test. I was shocked. I told her I had a test in March. I also said, "Isn't it medically wrong to test a person who already had it because it would not only come out positive but could cause serious medical problems for just taking the test?" She said, "Yes, I was given the wrong information about you." That was the problem. Everything about me in the federal system was all wrong.

That evening a Jamaican inmate with one and a half legs was put in the cell with me, but he slept on the floor. He was very seasoned, down eight years with twelve to go and all were about drugs. He was being transferred to another facility. He said he was framed by the government. After two nights and a written complaint to the marshals office downstairs, the London magistrate's order to have me forthwith in N.J. was not being carried out and that I was falsely being imprisoned. On the morning of the 24th day of July, 1996, I had a wake-up call at 4:30 AM. I was brought downstairs but was not allowed to put back on my street clothes. I had to keep prison clothes. Because I was being transported, I had to be dressed as the others on the plane and not with street clothes I came in with two days ago. I was told by the guards that on the 22nd I should not have traveled to Oklahoma in street clothes, but there was no way any change of clothes was available on the plane. They did tell me my clothes would be traveling with me, but the marshals would have them.

I departed from Kentucky at 8:30 AM after sitting in the wheelchair in the holding cell for four hours and with about thirty people. I arrived at Stewart Air Force Base in New York, then was driven for two hours to the county jail in N.J., stopping only once to exhale, arriving at 4:30 PM. Remember that marshal who told me what the magistrate had said on February 13 as I was being on my way out from the county jail to Kentucky, and also that my attorney wanted his name that I refused to give? Well, he was one of the marshals that picked me up at Stewart Air Force Base. I said to him, "Boy, I am glad to see you." He smiled as usual and replied, "To see me!" "Yes, I said," for I knew I was almost home, but least did I know it would be about another week before I was finally home.

My humiliation and demagoguery had to continue a little longer to the very last day. So I don't forget, I did not see the broken wing on the plane from Oklahoma. The marshal crew were the same. After sitting for two hours in cold concrete enclosure, I was finally processed and placed in the medical unit. While waiting to be processed, I called Patricia to let her know I made it back but not quite home. At least I was in New Jersey. I wanted to thank her for taking all my collect calls over the months and especially for going through all that trouble. Missing her doctor's appointment and all and that I would see her soon. Her niece recognizing my voice accepted the collect call and said, "Auntie Patricia died today, about a few hours ago in the hospital." I froze. Lord, I was hurt so bad. I did not get the chance to see her in person, to hold her and I blamed the government for purposely delaying my return. Had I left Kentucky when I had a plane ticket, I would have seen her and the government would have saved thousands. But it did not care about money; its mission had to be carried out by the evil doers.

Next day, July 25th, I was awaken at 4:30 AM and kept downstairs again in cold concrete enclosure until 9:45 AM, when a few inmates and I left for Fort Dix BOP and for Trenton court appearance. We took off with the same two marshals that picked me up in New York and we drove to Fort Dix, N.J., where a few of the prisoners were dropped off to serve their sentences. From the publication of February 1996 that I mentioned earlier, Fort Dix housed the largest amount of prisoners under the Bureau of Prisons system. Most of them are not from N.J. I recall one guy at Frankfurt, who was being taken back to North Carolina, to appear in court on a detainer after just finishing his sentence at Fort Dix N.J. He had even volunteered that when he spoke to his lawyer from the jail, he would ask him to contact the marshal service in Kentucky due to my ill health because he was upset that I could hardly walk when he saw me step out of my cell to go take a bath and how I dragged my feet to ambulate.

I sat in the van quiet for about twenty minutes, then respectfully asked the marshal what we were waiting for, and he replied that I was being picked up by Trenton marshals. I asked him "For what?" He replied that I would be seeing a judge in Trenton as far as he knew. I stepped out of the van, and one of the Trenton marshals asked the Newark marshal "is he jailable" because he took one look at me. I was taken to the Camden county jail and the marshals left, but not before one of them said, "I think you are in the wrong place and you will be taken back tomorrow in Newark." I could not believe it, but I knew who was behind all this. It was all intended for me to suffer before I get home. The prison guard took me in the spread eagle room, the usual thing but he did not go through it, not because he was black, but he looked at me, hardly walking and with a back brace. He would have to get me a chair to sit and start taking my clothes off. He asked me, "What happen? What did you do?" I told him and then he said to me, "You will win."

I was taken upstairs and held in a four-by-six cell with another guy with no room to move. After five hours of waiting, I was processed with the mug shots and all. I was placed in the jail's medical unit, which was very filthy and horrible. There were about ten people and as always there is the bully who has his bunk right by the public phone where he spends the longest time. He would remind others at times that he had to use the phone in the event it seemed they were on it too long, meaning five minutes tops. In the bathroom, green water was coming up the shower drain. The floor was slimy in the whole bath area. I took no bath.

The bully liked to keep the whole area dark when he looked at TV sitting at the other end of the area and away from him. His bunk is by the entrance door. That's where the light switch was. The Olympics were still on. I liked the swimmer from South Africa. She was hungry, dark tanned, though she was white, but had the reasonance feeling of aphrodisiac, which she conveyed to me since I first saw her at Frankfurt, KY.

On Friday, July 26th at 7:45 AM, I was told to get ready to leave. I was taken downstairs and put into a holding cage with about fourteen other people and no room to move. About nine, two different marshals came and got me. They said that there was a mix up and I did not belong in Trenton, so they drove me back the hour-long drive to the Newark courthouse, but before we took off, one of the marshals said to me, "We are not going to put any cuffs on you, but if you try anything I will beat the hell out of you." He should have taken a look at my feet. I wore rubber slippers since February 13th. They knew I was sick anyway. The veins running from my ankle to my toes could be vividly seen. I lost a lot of fluid in the foot. I was down to my last strength to walk. As I sat in the back seat of the car, the driver said to me, "I thought you were flying in from Kentucky yourself." This made me angry because this was how it should have been. I had my ticket and all but I was facing a personal quest by the plaintiff.

As we walked into the marshals area of the courthouse, which declines towards below ground level with one marshall in front of me with the leg irons and cuffs in his hands, the head marshal said, "What the, oh, him," for he remembered and recognized me back in February. It is the usual rule that all persons be kept in irons during transportation. I sat in the cell thinking what the marshal had said in the car about me returning to N.J. by myself. I said to myself that I would have been home, but somebody did not want me to get on the plane and return by myself. No, they did not want that to happen and like I said I knew who that was. The prosecutor could not see me getting off a plane in Newark, N.J. back on July 11th, because it would look too victorious for me, so he made sure I suffer by informing authorities in London, KY that I was a flight risk, just like he said back in January at my conditional bail hearing release. At that time he exaggerated "he is in debt, he has no job, and he has lost his real estate license." Later I would be apprised from the transcript of the July 10 hearing for my release that the government intended to inflict pain on me before I ever see New Jersey again.

I sat in the cell from10:25 AM till 2:30 PM when I was told that the prosecutor said he could not get in touch with my lawyer that day about my appearance representation, so my appearance would be on Monday, the 29th, just as was planned back on July. They got what they wanted, that was to have me paraded all over America under the marshal's custody to the day of my official appearance, all the time I suffered. I was taken back to the county jail and processed as usual. Since my ordeal began, I was processed some twenty times under the criminal justice system. I may need to check for radiation because it all happened within eighteen months.

I spent the weekend at county jail in Elizabeth, N.J., which by now kind of got tired seeing me. The guard remarked, "I thought we got rid of you." When I was brought down to the court house that Friday and was sitting in the cell, my Samaritan marshal walked by to the next cell to get someone and he said to me, "What you're doing here? Are you not supposed to be in Trenton? I took you there only yesterday." I told him I did not know, then he continued, "Leave it up to me for what you are going through. I would just drop you off at your house." I was very grateful that this guy always showed that he cared.

My lawyer drove all the way from Connecticut to see me that Saturday morning. He told me that he knew there was no court for me that Friday, the day before, for the prosecutor discussed it with him, that he the prosecutor did not have it fixed in his schedule and there was no way he could have told me if I called him. I could not call him nor him see me because I was constantly being moved about when I got to New Jersey. On Monday, July 29, 1996, I appeared in front of that same magistrate at 2:30 PM. I could see they all wanted the satisfaction to see me humiliated. The magistrate positioned his chair at right angle away from me looking at him. In other words, he seemed as if he was looking at the wall while speaking and he said this about me: "He got himself in trouble because of what he did and did not say to the probation and pre-trial." I knew he could not face me. I thought ,thought, *"I got myself in trouble because he said so and not probation nor pre-trial."* I could see the guilt in his face. He was right about one thing. What I did not say to probation was what probation stated in the PSR, and what I did say was left out.

The next day, my doctor got the June 21 bone scan results from the University of Kentucky hospital. On July 31, 1996, and one year from the date I first visited my rheumatologist, he gave me the stunning results from that bone scan taken a month and a half ago. I had severe bone disease and a collapsed arch in my left foot, which I believed was enhanced by wearing those rubber slippers for six months.

I finally got my hands on the transcript of July 10, 1996 hearing in Trenton. I have always felt that something went wrong that day that started the suffering I went through those several weeks. I was correct. Back in December 1995, in his objection response motions to have the evidentiary hearing to withdraw the illegal guilty plea, the prosecutor had remarked that I was a malingerer and that I manipulate the medical community, and now on July 10, 1996, he said "the defendant suffers from a well documented history of infirmities and he would need a special type of transportation, like an ambulance. The government has such transportation." I sure in hell did not get what he said. What I got was being thrown into county jails across America and left to survive under the mercies of God. He was very convincing to the judge just as he did in the past and he got the court's blessing to carry the assault against me. When I was being taken from London to Frankfurt, KY on July 12, the tobacco-chewing marshal remarked, "Makes no sense, instead of a what it is, $300 plane trip, now it will cost thousands before you can get back to New Jersey." But the government did not care about the money, only my hide. The evil doers had to carry out their mission.

Thank God for my N.J. physicians. I was at the end of my rope. I went through several tests. Immediately, I was given narcotics to abate and control the pain. Medication was constantly upgraded. My leg was put into a cast by another physician for several weeks and I had to wear special canvas shoes. It took at least six months before I could wear shoes again.

Today, my legs are much better than a year ago. But the legal fight is not over yet. When discovery material came to light, I learned from the paper trail along with my inexperienced contributions how much evil was levied against me at any cost so the government could win. After I returned home, I had six months of mail to go through. First, I found out that the union gave in and I lost my job, next, my voting rights were taken away and my real estate license revoked. The government wasted no time for conviction, which was illegal from the get go. Finally, I discovered that my house was under foreclosure and I had substantial debt.

Anarchy and Social Unrest

Although we should never condone anarchy, albeit it had not only been a strong force but a catalyst to freedom for people in many countries around the world, especially in Europe and Africa, anarchy has restored democratic societies that were once dictatorship, hobbesean and less egalitarian societies. After decades of totalitarianism by the Soviet Union, the people were not going to take it anymore from a society that an American president once called an evil empire. There were years of fighting in Afghanistan and the resistances in the Baltic States crushed by the soviets, but by the will of the people, they kept pressing on and many of them paid with their lives for change.

There were recently, a few years ago, a large demonstration in Tiananmen Square in Beijing, China where scores of lives were lost; crushed to death. The biggest, largest achievement for change came at the end of the 1980s when the Berlin Wall fell, but before that happened, many east Berliners who defied the east German government suffered death and destruction when hundreds of them were killed for attempting to seek freedom on the other side of the wall to the west. Anarchy was necessary in these circumstances.

America's kind of anarchy is more like social unrest. Many Americans cried about how wrong America was to get into the war with Vietnam that lasted many years and took many lives. Americans at home burnt the American flag as a symbol of their disbelief about the war, while others said the war brought wealth and prosperity to the country, which people felt was only capitalism taking its place in America while our boys were dying. Americans not only burnt flags, but they also marched in protest and many of them got killed for what they believed in, just like those students in Tiananmen Square in China.

In the 1990s, there came about a different kind of social unrest in America. People began to lose faith and confidence in their government. They demonstrated their resentments against certain areas of the government, and law enforcement was one of those areas. Some of the people resented the law enforcement agencies. The tragedy at Waco, Texas in 1992 made Americans feel overwhelmed that their government's only concern was effective force instead of negotiating peace. Dozens of lives, many of them children, could have been saved. Instead the government carried out a command raid against the people in that compound where just about everyone was killed. The government also lost a few of their agents, though their lives were just as important as those in the compound, it was a small percentage that was in no way in contrast to the larger population that lost their lives. Some said the government's agents were very insensitive.

Then there were the Freemen which many people thought was an organization with a just cause. The Freemen were a group of people who set themselves up at a Montana area and their beliefs were that the government's concerns were above those and not in the best interest of the people. They picked up arms to defend their beliefs according to the constitution and held law enforcement officers at bay for several weeks before they gave up. Some people were shocked that others had the guts to stand up against the American government. Although the standoff ended, it was clear that the message got across. The people had cried out with the hope that it would not be another Waco and it worked. There were no incidents.

Then there was the Militia springing up all over the country vowing to pick up arms to defend what their beliefs were, and one of those beliefs were that America was losing its values to protect and serve the people's cultural, social and economic rights. A survey of the people showed that some were uncomfortable, while others started believing and supporting the cause of this new breed of anarchists. This was clear at the prison in Lexington. Some of the inmates followed the Freemen and the Militia story every day on TV, and even took notes for others who were not present during the broadcasts. I overheard emotions of hate and disbelief in their government, about things done to them and other people they know not incarcerated.

Then there was the Ruby Ridge, Idaho incident where an innocent person was shot cold to death by a government agent sniper. This enraged the people at such a behavior by their own government and after several years, in August 1997, the government said it was charging its agent for the wrongful death of that Ruby Ridge woman. Through the years, her family must have endured the pain that many of us may never know unless we were in their same situation.

The Oklahoma City bombing was no excuse that people were mad at the government, but that was the very reason why it happened according to reports. It was horrible and no matter how mad you are at your government officials, there are no justification to kill harmless innocent women and children. This incident to me was the highest form of social unrest because it took lives of a city and a nation and shook them all to pieces.

So far, as I know, the World Trade Center catastrophe in New York City was caused by foreigners, but still the act contributed to the social unrest in America because when something of this magnitude occurs, it affects all of us.

The Prosecutor

Guilty at Any Cost

In the preceding chapters, you have seen how the prosecution was hell bent for a conviction against me even if it was an illegal one. All that mattered was another notch in the belt of a prosecutor whether they be federal, state or local, and they are supposed to abide by ethical rules but most of them do not because of their quest to win. Under title 28:547 of the USCA (United States Code Annotated), the United States attorneys known as federal prosecutors are supposed to perform their duties honestly and fairly as a rule, but some of them do not.

A prosecutor has a sovereign obligation in the court room to govern with impartiality; therefore, his job is not that it should win a case, but justice shall be done. He must not try to win cases by using tactical, calculated and improper methods; instead, he should use every legitimate means to bring about a just conviction. He must not violate the oath he had sworn to uphold when he took office.

In many prosecution processes, deals are made, such as to plea guilty for a lesser sentence. Not that it would save money as they often say, because they were sure not concerned about money in the quest towards my destruction. You see, a plea of guilty assures the government of a conviction without even trying to get one in a court of law, and the convicted party would never have known that if he or she had went to trial, the outcome could have been different. This concept of pleading guilty is most consistent with those who are poor and of minority backgrounds due to the expense and the cost of legal defense. Public defenders who are always in constant rush to get the charged individual to plea guilty as his best way out are playing right into the hands of the prosecutor. This happened to me. However, the convicted person is scarred for life and with a conviction on his record he is viewed as being damaged forever.

Then there is the negotiating plea for a lesser sentence no matter what the severity of the crime is, because the government wants information in exchange so that the prosecution can prosecute another with that information. I call this blackmail in the criminal justice system. Although it might have worked in the war against violent crimes and corruption, it is still wrong to get justice this way.

One of the worst kind of examples of guilty at any cost was when a prominent New York crime boss of the alleged Gambino crime family was brought down by his own man. This man pled guilty to nineteen murders with consequent disclosure of an additional six murders totaling twenty-five. The government was not interested in those murders and how the families would be affected for generations; all they wanted was the top man, the alleged godfather who they tried to prosecute for years but was always unsuccessful, so the only way for them to succeed was to actually overlook a confession of the murders of many just for the conviction of one man. This conviction of the alleged godfather was of a greater conquest than of the confession to the murders of many. This enraged the people when they found out about the unforgivable evil behind the deal. This even enraged the Mafia boys back at the big house about such a deal that lacked the stamina of a Mafiosa, who never sings. Never could I have ever understood how something like this is allowed to happen in our supposedly civilized world, but after listening to other people's stories in the small house (county jails), and the big house, and reading newspapers, not to mention my own experience, then I finally understood why.

The answer is conquest. To convict a person like the alleged New York crime boss was more like a personal victory for the prosecutor. He could even have state and national fame to bring down the *Teflon Don*. To hell with the confessed murders. They are not important. In the concessions made with the government for such a big prize, the informant was placed into the government witness protection program. This particular informant was given a little time in prison, but it was no ordinary prison. He had all his luxuries as if he were at home according to news sources. He was not deprived of anything like a free person, except perhaps going to the beach or to parties, but even these activities I am not sure of. Oh, before I forget, he was allowed to keep his millions. The witness protection program provides informants with new identities and relocations to other areas of the country to live out their lives.

In another incident, in 1984 a man facing 195 years in prison for smuggling marijuana became a government informant, so he could turn his associates in. He got eight years instead at a time when only one-third had to be served. He was allowed to keep his $20 million, and his wife, also an accomplice, was never prosecuted. This information and more was documented in the May 1996 edition of the Erie daily times.

In a May 1997 TV broadcast of prosecutorial misconduct, the prosecution's star witness who had stated that she did not have on her contact lens nor her glasses, which she admitted was a definite disadvantage for her to see who actually did the shooting that killed her fiancée, while they were walking down a Louisiana street. She said she had made that statement to the police, but the prosecutor kept this information from the trial and a sixteen-year-old black kid was sentenced to death for something he has constantly denied he did not do. A videotape proved that he was playing basketball some distance away from the scene just before the murder.

An excellent example of a prosecutor's quest to convict was that of the late Somerset County, New Jersey prosecutor, who demonstrated havoc and mayhem in the county with his blatant violation, abuse and misuse of power within the criminal justice system by making illegal deals, violating forfeiture laws, squandering funds and acquiring ill-gotten guilty pleas. The bottom line is, who suffers from it all? We do, the poor and the helpless. With the ordinary man or woman who is poor and does not have much, only the Lord can help him or her if he or she is ever convicted. He can be expected to serve long prison terms and years of servitude in the government prison industries and earning just pennies a day in a cruel criminal justice system that is secular in treatment even behind bars due to privilege and prejudice.

Moreover, when any person is found guilty and convicted, he is no longer treated like a human being. He becomes fair game for prejudice, persecution and ridicule, but for the government, their bottom line is that they got their man, no matter what the cost was and death is no exception.

The Haves and the Havenots

Justice in America, whether criminal or civil for a defendant, the decision is predicated upon status, physical appearance, race, gender and affiliation within the society. In the past few decades, we were promised that we would not be discriminated anymore with words like national origin, sex, ancestry, color, etc. The awful truth is that justice is delivered based upon all the above and more that doesn't fit ordinary morals to be mentioned on paper, but have been well demonstrated in our society.

In other words, bias and prejudice play pivotal roles in the eyes of the police and others who are supposed to enforce the law. As I write this page at this moment, there is an ongoing investigation of severe brutality in New York City against a Haitian immigrant who sustained such severe internal injuries that he may forever have difficulty to relieve human waste due to damaged to his bladder and rectum. This outrageous act of destruction of life and limb shocked the nation. The law is the law, but the law is how different judges interpret and view the law. The judge instructs the facts to the court and the jury determines the level of sentences. Then there is the jury which could be very frightening for they determine guilt or innocence. A jury has the power to do us the greatest harm or the greatest good depending on all the appearance factors described above.

The have and the havenots are those people whose justices are based solely on the effects of privilege, bias and prejudice. In court proceedings, judges can make decisions whether they like or don't like someone. A judge's decision could send a person to prison, pauperize him and can even put him in the streets (homeless) because he has lost everything due to that judge's decision. Many times there is judicial oversight, which could also be categorized as discretionary power, but lawyers do not fight back hard enough because of fear of retaliation in the court room in the future. His client is taken away in shackles and he can only hope for relief on appeal, which is decided by another judge. In the meantime, the injured party, the defendant, is suffering.

There are judges who may think someone is guilty before he is found guilty. In this country you are supposed to be presumed innocent by everyone and anyone until you are convicted by a jury. Even at the time of arrest, a person is absolutely beyond any doubt presumed innocent, but some judges feel that when a person is arrested, indicted, detained or released on bail, he is probably guilty. Bail could be a critical process for a defendant, and prejudice could play a great part. Bail should not be intended to punish someone or to be used as a method to keep him locked up until trial. The reason for bail is to ensure a person will show up in court. Factors determining bail are levels of offense, criminal history, financial and family situations, roots in the community, and the likelihood that the person will show up on his court date.

One of the most privileged bails I have been informed as I write this story was about a sixty-year-old white male and former state Democratic Party chairman, who was arrested outside a motel with possession of crack cocaine. He was released on $250 bail. He was allowed to attend a thirty-day in-patient program, and since it was his first offense, the judge said that he would be most likely qualified for a conditional discharge. This shocked me. I remember meeting this eighteen-year-old black kid at the federal court holding cell back in February just before my long visit down south. This kid pled guilty to his first offense. He was facing fifteen years if convicted at trial and his mother was putting up her house for bail until he returned for sentencing in sixty days. He is probably doing his servitude at a federal prison somewhere in America far away from home.

Remember when my illegal misdemeanor conviction was vacated and on release I was arrested at the federal prison by marshals? A $60,000 bail was demanded because I was recharged on the same misdemeanor charge and I still had a zero criminal history even to this day, as I am writing this chapter more than a year later. Addressing these cases of bail, one would most likely conclude that race, color, status, roots, affiliations, etc., play the pivotal role between the haves and the havenots. Had a person of color caught with crack cocaine, he would not be allowed into an in-patient care program and a conditional discharge. He could expect a conviction and a jail term for certain.

With the American president attending the 27th Annual Legislative Conference of the Congressional Black Caucus Foundation in September 1997, black representatives put aside their differences for one night about concerns of how blacks receive unfair drug sentencing and education. In the past several years, it had been of great concern that the guideline of stiffer mandatory sentences by the federal government Sentencing Commission for the possession of crack cocaine versus powdered cocaine unfairly discriminate against black offenders.

Another example of bail privilege was that of a forty-four-year-old white postal worker facing a maximum of 423 years if convicted, for having a cache of assault weapons in his apartment. He was released on $2,500 or ten percent of his $25,000. Bail, in both of these cases, cocaine and weapons, falls under the violent crime category. To be sentenced for a crime in America, you can become fair game for destruction or you can be given another chance in life, all depending on who or what you are. Here are some examples of preferential treatment:

1. A convicted Alabama governor was sentenced to five years probation, fined $212,000 (which he could probably afford), and had to serve 1000 hours service. In June 1997, he was pardoned by the parole board of (3) members, two of which were appointed by him when he was in office, the other was appointed by his successor.

2. A $67,000-a-year N.J. fire captain was given probation instead of a ten-year sentence for selling dog food in his store

when the food was supposed to be donated to the society for the prevention of cruelty to animals.

3. A Pennsylvania franchise shop-in-the-bag store owner was sentenced to three years probation after pleading guilty to mail fraud, tax evasion, and illegally cashing $160,000 of unused manufacturer coupons, which he illegally obtained when he made a deal with a dog owner of 600 abandoned animals to give him all her unused dog food manufacturer coupons, which he cashed in. He also coerced his employees to write nice letters about him to the court and even threatened to withhold payments to his employees' pension fund although the money is deducted from their paychecks.

For a federal judge to overlook the blackmailing by the defendant to his employees and still give this man a sentence of probation, it is inconceivable, but of course this guy had status, white, and was in a privileged position.

4. A N.J. school district administrator facing five years in prison and $30,000 fine for forgery was put in the pre-trial intervention program (PTI) recommended for first-time offenders, where upon completion the charges are ultimately dropped. The report also stated that the maximum conviction could have been just three years of probation and full restitution.

5. A New Jersey state police sergeant, after serving five months on a six-year sentence for $500,000 fraud, tampering and falsifying records, walked out of prison and was allowed into the same pre-trial intervention program. The report said that he would be doing some community service and subjection to curfews and routine telephone checks.

I have never heard about any person of color that had such a break as these two. They were both state employees.

6. A former I.R.S agent in Florida, who laundered $100 million for drug dealing, forfeited none of his assets after joining the government witness protection program.

These are some of the examples of the softer approach that some convicted criminals receive for doing serious crimes. The havenots, including myself, have been mentioned in just about every page in this story. The following are a few other examples:

7. A former black panther jailed for twenty-seven years was released in June of 1997 in Orange, California after it was discovered that the prosecution star witness was an infiltrator and paid informant for the (FBI) and the police. The man was serving a life sentence.

8. A New Jersey man, after serving ten years on a fifty-year sentence for rape, was freed through *habeas corpus* in June 1995, when a federal judge ruled that the defense lawyer made serious errors that deprived him a fair trial.

9. A white thirty-four-year-old Missouri man spent twelve years in prison on a ninety-year sentence for sexual assault on an eighty-two-year-old woman, and all the time confessing his innocence. His conviction was thrown out in May 1995 and he was ordered either released or retried. Knowing how the government's revenge of vindictiveness works, he was released on $50,000 bond in February 1997, almost two years later, but died one week later after his release. The report stated that he died from a heart attack brought on by stress.

This was a case that went wrong from the very start and this man never had the opportunity to clear his name.

I believe that every person should be given the appropriate punishment for his crime. I hope that the reader does understand that I do not condone any crime, but when the punishment and treatment of one is discriminated as to the punishment and treatment of another because of race, gender, status and all the bias features mentioned at the beginning of this chapter, then we as Americans must stand up together and fight for what is right and not get into the trap of the evil doers.

Redemption

It is of great concern when government uses its penal laws to punish its citizens, intentionally to cause them harm and inflict emotional distress on them. For generations, many people have suffered and are still suffering for just being who they are or what they have become. One of the greatest injustices to many of these people is mainly because of racism, whether it was closet racism as experienced in the north, or overt racism expressed in the American deep south.

Recently, in the summer of 1997, the United States president, in a response to his race relations' objectives, publicly apologized to the descendants and the few still alive Tuskegee Alabama black airmen for the injustices they received while serving their country during the Second World War. These black airmen were not only denied proper medical care as their white counterpart, but they were purposely neglected for their great contributions to the war because, as usual, they and all blacks were still considered less than full, regular normal beings as was the order of the day during America's sinful past of black slavery for hundreds of years. Though the apology came more than fifty years late, it was still welcomed as relief and some kind of closure to the remaining families of those Tuskegee airmen.

Soon after the president's apology, the people cried out that the president should go further and apologize to the nation for the centuries of wrongs America has done to its black citizens.

Surprisingly, a bill introduced some time ago, and by at least one white congressman, had suggested that this national apology was necessary. After hearing about such an apology in the making, some whites responded that such an apology could result in extensive reparations and that they should not carry the guilt and the wrongs of their forefathers, but the truth is that the wrongs still exist in about every branch of America's institutions. Some whites might have seen this apology as the fulfillment of Dr. Martin Luther King's legacy and his mountaintop dream that if America was to live up to the true meaning of its creed, then it must be prepared to embrace all of us as one in a nation under God.

What they should understand is that African Americans have confronted a legacy of slavery, segregation, discrimination and racism, and it is quite obvious that America owes recompense for its past deeds against African Americans. By failing to treat them fairly in times of trouble and misfortunes, it reinforces black feelings of isolation and encouragers black separatism. What many people misunderstand is that a public apology by one for the action of millions would give acknowledgement that the wrongs done to African Americans have finally been recognized, which could ease their pains and start the healing process that would give them horizons of hope for their future and the future of their generations.

There had been reparations in the past, such as those paid to Japanese in American camps and a much larger reparation by Germany after the armistice at the end of the Second World War for the wrongs committed in Europe. But African Americans do not want money for America's wrongs; they need to restore hope and the opportunity to be in equation to America's whites.

All people of color must be treated equally, but the American criminal justice system does not. Authority of criminal law should not be used to punish citizens through economic regulations. Penal laws have been used to deprive persons of property through severe fines. It can deprive a person his liberty and even his life. I have touched on all of these factors in my story where people have lost their property like myself and their life like that of the guy who died of a heart attack, looking at the fight back then on

TV while I was in prison, and the Missouri man in the previous chapter. A defendant should not be sent to prison for rehabilitation.

Imprisonment is punishment. To confine someone for his affliction than his benefaction is not an agreeable act in a civilized society. Someone like myself (though my conviction was illegal) and the eighty-two-year-old New York doctor who have given decades of service to the poor, and not excluding thousands of others who are not dangerous, should not be confined in order to incapacitate us. It is most probable that they will not commit similar offenses again. If someone must be imprisoned for valid reasons, then the criminal justice system should seek to make rehabilitative sources available to him or her. But the goal of rehabilitation cannot fairly serve in itself as grounds for the sentence to confinement, at the same time serving the government's purpose of slave labor producing lucrative rewards.

Conclusion

The United States of America, a great country as it is with wealth and might, should never allow enforcers of its laws to abuse those laws. Neither should it benefit from the advantages of its criminal justice systems nor of the disadvantages of the poor and the prejudiced through authority of its criminal laws.

Immigrants like myself and those decades before me look to America as a beacon of hope, but unfortunately, some of us become victims of misfortune at some point of our lives, but that does not mean we should be treated as *unequals* because we look, speak, and sound different than the millions that came before us. The problem is that those millions before some of us now were rather homogeneous by race. Then why does America say at its libraries, museums, and airports its long- ago doctrine, "Give me your tired, your poor, your huddled masses yearning to breathe free. Send these, the homeless, tempest-tossed to me. I lift my lamp besides the golden door."

Who do these famous words refer to? You? Me? Every and anybody? Oh, no, I don't think so.

Before my accident and my misfortunes, I was interested to serve America as an ambassador. I wrote letters to the president and my congressman just about a few months before my injury. I still felt I could recover early to pursue that objective, but I was wrong. I would have liked very much to follow the footsteps of the former presidential candidate Shirley Chisholm, who became

U.S ambassador to Jamaica. I think it was the land of her origin. Had I succeeded, it would not have been just as much but much more of what was portrayed by the legendary actor Sidney Poitier about an immigrant from the same country of my birth, who went to England and transformed the lives of a few.

Yes, it would have been much more because I would not be representing just a few, but the ideas of millions. I would have been America's very own "To Sir, with Love."

www.ingramcontent.com/pod-product-compliance
Lightning Source LLC
Chambersburg PA
CBHW060635290526
45793CB00001B/257